MY SKELETONS HAVE NAMES

HOW I WENT FROM VICTIM TO HERO

SHARI LUECK

Legal Disclaimer

Published by: Shari Lueck
ISBN: 978-0-578-79266-8

Praise For My Skeletons Have Names

"Shari Lueck is a true survivor. Her story provides a model to others learning to tap into the hero within."

Dr. Amy Ellis – Development and Growth Strategist

"Shari's description of her own trauma illustrates to the reader that anything can be overcome. So much of what she describes will resonate with readers that are struggling with abandonment issues, shame and not feeling good enough. Shari shares morsels of wisdom throughout this book and gives the reader hope that they too can overcome whatever pain they have experienced."

Shannone Bhote – HR Director

"Shari Lueck writes with authenticity and passion about a difficult and personal story. *My Skeletons Have Names* will linger with readers long after they close the cover."

Tracey Bradley – Writer/Producer

Shari Lueck

"I had the luck to meet and connect with Shari a few years ago on our quest to heal. Since then I have had moments where Shari has shown up with her words and spirit that shine on my soul. Now I understand why. The book allowed me to know what her soul resonates with mine and how to heal the parts to get to the level of mental health and healing that Shari has. I was left wanting more. This is and going to be helpful for so many."

Shana McDonald – Yoga Instructor

"Shari's open and heartfelt sharing of her story compels the reader to take a fearless look at her or his own experiences of trauma. The gifts offered in this book are strength, healing and hope from a brave and compassionate woman."

S. J. Schickofke

"The lessons you teach and the wisdom you share in this book from your journey are raw, brave, and bold. They are what we need more of in this world.

We all have had struggles, challenges, and bad experiences. We're human and we don't know what we're doing so we make tons of mistakes. The problem- we all want to pretend they didn't happen. We want to hide our skeletons in shame and fear. Instead, Shari uses her life to uncover, acknowledge, and face those skeletons. It's given her enormous power which she has chosen to use to teach others how to dance with their skeletons and be free of shame. Something so many of us don't even realize is the root of our issues.

This book manages to leave me feeling raw and vulnerable while at the same time wrapped in love, safe and secure ready to embrace my own life. Dare I say my own skeletons?"

Tammy Collins – Award winning Graphic Designer & Brand Marketing expert

"This book is a testament to how if you face your fears and the skeletons we have, you can overcome anything. Shari writes from an authentic place of pain, but she also shares her joy in her transformation. She gives us insight into her life and how she decided that she was going to fight for the life she and her children deserved. All of us have skeletons and to deny that we don't is doing ourselves and the people we could touch a disservice. However, it takes bravery to uncover and name them. Shari did just that and now she's inspiring others to do that same. This book is for anyone struggling with past issues that still affect them today. It's written from a place of authenticity and love."

LaKisha Mosley – Lifestyle & business Blogger & Top-Rated podcast Host

"My Skeletons Have Names discusses tips and is an educational self-help and leadership guide that facilitates change. Shari's self-improvement book includes thought-provoking prompts and tools for effecting change in a wide range of situations.

The book's invitation to think differently, innovate regularly, and "meet your skeletons" resiliently after encountering stumbling blocks is based on her many decades of experience with dealing with addiction, guilt, and pain—experiences that she says came at a cost. In a frank and conversational tone, she shares descriptions of personal hurdles, including unanticipated unemployment, inappropriate behavior from bosses, and drug addiction. These anecdotes give credence to the book's suggestions for unloading the weighty baggage left by unsettling experiences.

Through detailed discussions and tips for confronting personal and professional challenges, *My Skeletons Have Names* is an educational self-help and leadership guide that facilitates manageable change with boundary-breaking tools."

Daniella Park – Best Selling Author

"You've given me hope beyond my wildest dreams to know if you can survive the trauma and abuse of your past

I can too. No one should ever have to experience such abuse and trauma as Shari has in her life from those that were there to love, cherish and protect her.

This book is a "must read" if you are ready to go from "victim to hero" in your own life. The "ARC" methodology she writes about will walk you through recognizing, admitting, reviewing and the ability to rewrite your own story. What an amazing concept, we can rewrite and recreate our futures to be full of the love and happiness that we've only dreamed of until now.

As victims, we often settle for the love we think we deserve. Once we think we deserve better, we get better. Wow! That's very powerful! Shari is a beautiful and amazing young woman that I truly feel blessed to have in my life as a friend and as my life coach. "

Glenda Acevedo – Business Development Manager

"I must say I was hooked after reading the first twenty-five pages sent to me. I could not put it down. Her writing had me going through the motions and struggles alongside her and had me rooting for her recovery and success. She was so raw and open and yet so positive. I could feel the fight for her life through her words. Honestly, I wanted more. Well done."

Christina Garcia

Shari Lueck

"Vulnerability at its finest. Shari is both informative and inspiring. She taught me that 'You accept the love you think you deserve and reject the love that you think you do not deserve.' Extremely insightful. "

Nicole Busino

"What a great read, brave authenticity throughout each page! I am inspired, filled with gratitude and grounded with the power shared with your book.

Thank you."

Tanjanika Latrell

"What a fascinating and insightful read! This book is a testament to the promise that when traumatic events happen to us and we change our behaviors as a strategy to deal with pain and fear and to protect ourselves there can also be a time when that changes and we have a new path to transformative healing and growth that ripples out to the world and changes things for the better.

This happens when and if one is willing to engage in the work of excavating the core sacred self (the light of who you really are) from the wreckage of internalized guilt, externalized blame, developmental trauma and limiting beliefs. It takes courage and tenacity—Shari has both in abundant supply.

I also celebrate that Shari endorses the idea that not everything happens for a reason and that we can be empowered by our past fears to break through to a new way of being!

As a woman, I am encouraged by the resilience Shari exhibits and explains in her book, not just rising from and utilizing her painful past but she transforms it into a fuel that moves her into her higher purpose to help others heal.

I'm impressed at her ability and her drive to concentrate it into a written prologue, particularly in a time when as a nation we are in chaos and so many people are in need of direction and guidance for healing.

As a mental health professional, I recognize how the tools identified in this book are key to moving forward from the past and showing up in your present-day life more in alignment with your true values and your highest intentions. Undoubtedly the relationship with God/Source/Higher Power is key to her path.

Thankfully the advances and ability to understand and treat complex PTSD has come much further in the past ten years and trauma sensitivity is more prevalent in the medical communities, so that they can dovetail with the methods that Shari outlines.

I would encourage anyone struggling with a difficult past to read this book, and to begin to apply some simple (but not always easy) instruction. I will recommend this book and these tools to my clients and others who are on a similar journey."

With appreciation and joy, C. Delene Cole, MS, LMFT –
Licensed Marriage and Family Therapist

"In this moving, honest, and inspiring memoir, Shari is nothing but frank in describing her experiences. Shari's voice and conversational exclamations ring loud and clear throughout as she describes how shame and blame came to impact her life in more ways than you can imagine.

Shari talks with such bravery about the dark experiences she encountered throughout her childhood. The feelings of fear, abandonment, sheer mental and physical abuse, little stability, and constant betrayal which all contributed to shaping her life experiences. She shares the details of her use of alcohol and substance misuse as a way to fit in socially.

Shari shares some brilliant strategies to help deal with shame that many of us have been exposed to, teaching us how to choose our happiness rather than living in the past, helping you to tap into the courage you have within you and how to create healthy boundaries that can help protect you.

My Skeletons Have Names allows the reader to absorb her trauma, whilst teaching you a way of accepting the past, which can lead to strengthening future possibilities."

Review Sue Cullen – Capabilities Coach

Dedication

To my children Jessica, Josh, and Danny who taught me what unconditional love is and gave me the courage to become who I was created to be.

To my husband for loving me exactly how I am.

To my parents for never giving up on me.

Table of Contents

Shari Lueck

Preface

I felt myself losing consciousness as my breath was choked out of me. I could see him holding the hammer in his left hand as he pulled tighter on the scarf he'd fastened around my neck. To be honest, I was used to the sensation of not being able to breathe, but this time was different; I knew that this time, I was going to die.

Part of me wanted to die. I was tired of this world and the lifetime of abuse and brutality I had lived. I have had my jaw broken, my eardrums busted, and more black eyes than I can count. I've had my mouth punched so hard that my front teeth chipped, and to this day, I cannot wear anything that gets close to or touches my neck because it reminds me of the sensation of hands wrapped around my throat, choking me.

In my mind, I deserved every blow I got and maybe, this time, it would be the last. As I gasped for air, I thought, okay, just let go and be over with it.

But…

My children. What would happen to them if I was gone? My love for them was greater than I had ever loved anything in my life. Each one was a miracle from God, and who would protect them if I was not there?

I saw their faces one more time as everything started to turn dark, but inside was a burning desire and a prayer that I would wake up one more time.

That moment was the turning point in my life, and I am so thankful that God gave me another chance. That was the beginning of my search for my true self, and the quest to become the person He had created me to be.

Who Are You?

Let me ask you a question: "Who are you?" I ask this question of many people I meet along the way and I always get the same answers; they tell me what they do for a living, their marital status, or that they are parents, and I smile because I know that is not the whole truth.

Then I look them in the eye and ask again, "Who are you, really?" They often give me a quizzical look or glance away because they cannot answer. They simply do not know.

How about you? Can you answer that question? Who are you, really?

Most people cannot, and if you are in that group of people, there is no shame in that. Society has told you for so long who you are, that somewhere along the way you lost your ability to recognize your true, authentic self.

This book will show you how that happened to you and how you can change that. You will learn to recognize who were you before the world told you who you were supposed to be, and before you started trying to modify yourself to fit in or get approval.

If you can answer that question and know who you truly are, then congratulations; you have done the deep work required. You will enjoy this book as I share my journey. You will see yourself in it and will probably learn some more about yourself and the people around you. It will become a tool to help others find the freedom you enjoy.

This book is about hope and how a life, even as messed up as mine, can be changed. You will be amazed at what I have survived, how many times I have faced death, and how God spared me because He had bigger plans.

I invite you to join me on a journey to freedom because on the other side of the skeletons in your closet, you will find abundant joy, and a successful life!

Shari Lueck

Introduction

Life has no limitations, except the ones that you make.
Les Brown

According to Wikipedia, **a skeleton in the closet** or **skeleton in the cupboard** is a colloquial phrase and idiom used to describe an undisclosed fact about someone which, if revealed, would damage perceptions of the person.

Can I share something with you? We all have skeletons; yes, even you. Some may be hiding in the closet, but all of them have left an imprint on your heart and live in the shadows of your soul. If you have lived on this earth long enough to become an adult, I promise you, they are there.

Our journey in life is a trail of experiences that we witness or things that happen to us. All of our experiences are a result, however, of our own choices and/or actions. In my lifetime, I have moved from victim to hero and from blame to accountability over and over again. A wise sage once told me, "Shari, the days are long and the years short," and as the years pass by, time feels like it is accelerating.

When you look at the span of a single year, so much changes. Reflecting, as I write this, the world does not remotely look the same as it did just a few months ago, never mind an entire year ago. Covid-19, a global pandemic is rising and has changed the way we all are accustomed to living life. One year ago, nobody could have predicted that our world would change in the blink of an eye. We were all living life as we had been for generations.

As I shared how days are long and years are short with a friend, she said to me, "Shari, one year ago today, I was not a grandma; one year ago, tomorrow, I was. Now my grandbaby is turning one. He has changed so much in this past year."

For all of us, this will be a year that will forever be ingrained in our memory. It has impacted us in ways we have yet to discover and will change us. For the children, they will remember how the school year was shortened and lessons were learned at home. All graduations were cancelled or postponed, and everyone had to practice social distancing. No longer were they able to see family or friends, play outside beyond their own backyard, or even go shopping with Mom or Dad. They are watching the world living in fear. What skeleton(s) will this leave in their memory? Only time will tell.

Not all of our skeletons are scary or hidden. However, most of the skeletons we have showed up in childhood, often as a result of judgement, and the words that assigned shame and blame became a part of our lives. Somewhere around the age of nine or ten, we started listening to society and the voices that told us how to act and what to be. The labels put us into categories, and we tried to figure out who we are, where we fit, and acted accordingly.

We begin to lose touch with our true and authentic self when we allow society to shape us. We can get trapped, and the surrender becomes too difficult. Shame, blame, and other excuses hold us back. As time passes, we hold on to our new identities and it becomes a vicious cycle that we cannot change. Does that sound familiar to you?

The subtle feelings of shame and blame cause us to want to hide our stories and the things that make us unique and who we are. Maybe you stole some change from your mom's dresser when you were little. You were told that was wrong and not to take things that do not belong to you. Then, when you were a little bit older, you did not return a book you borrowed. Again, you were counseled about stealing. Fast forward to your teen years and you got caught taking the car without permission. This time, your parents labeled you as a thief.

Your mom starts by saying: "Remember when you stole that dollar from me? I've known since then that you were a thief." This now becomes a character trait that you get associated with and you turn that trait into a whole story, fearful that people will think you are a thief. This dialogue creates a skeleton tied to a shameful emotion, which then may influence future decisions that you make.

I am going to share a secret with you. Many times, the skeletons you carry are the same ones your parents and grandparents hid away and did not talk about, both trauma & beliefs get passed down from generation to generation until they are faced, and something changes.

Each generation will reap what the former generation has sown.

Chinese Proverb

Everything we experience influences the way we live life. We have opportunities to change patterns or continue them. Some patterns we carry on knowingly, and some by default that seem to be stuck on the repeat cycle. Later in this book, I am going to share a story about my intuition and knowing in my gut, at a very young age, that my birth certificate father was not my biological father.

Interestingly, my mother had always suspected that her birth certificate father was not her biological father either. My DNA discovery led her to uncover that she too had been duped and her birth certificate father and biological father were not one in the same either.

Imagine the surprise when I called her to share my DNA results and let her know that, based on my DNA, she has some questions to answer beyond who is my biological dad? My mom listened and took the test. She was not surprised, but in shock to learn that her DNA led to a different lineage than the one she had spent 72 years believing. She said to me, "You don't know what it feels like." I was floored; of course, I knew exactly what that felt like. Sometimes, you just want to shake people. Crazy isn't it? You will learn that I have one bizarre story after another. I have survived more extraordinary circumstances than a cat has lives. You just cannot make this stuff up!

When I told my daughter about my findings and her grandmother's discovery, I said that I had good and bad news for her. I said, "The good news is your father is *your* father. The bad news is he is your father." We laughed and then realized I'd changed history and that was a big skeleton I am happy to put on a shelf.

How My Skeletons Took Life

Early on, the messages I got from my surroundings taught me not to listen to my gut and intuition, and that I should not trust my feelings. This led to self-doubt and a broken internal governor that led my self-regulating system to malfunction. Add abuse to the malfunction and misfires became a common occurrence. Abuse causes you to not know what is healthy or right, nor how to have proper boundaries because things happened to you beyond your control.

This creates conditioning where we may seek out psychological and emotional abuse from others because, subconsciously, we associate it with love or fulfillment. If this person shows you this type of attention or talks to you this way, then they must love or like you because that is how your family treats/treated you. It becomes a compulsive familiarity cycle where abusive behavior provides a sense of mastery or pleasure because you attribute it to what you think love feels like.

Over time, this can lead to feelings of helplessness, thinking you are crazy, that there's something wrong with you, or out of control behavior. In each cycle or chapter in life, you are dealing with things that reinforce the message that you are bad. Subconsciously, you continue to seek out what is familiar, hoping to ease those feelings, but it ultimately makes them worse.

Here is something to think about: You accept the love you think you deserve and reject the love that you think you do not deserve. I will let you ponder that one for a while.

When Does Healing Come?

When you get back in touch with your true and authentic self. Only then can you remove the shame and blame that you carry, and truly forgive yourself and others. Then you can create better boundaries in your life. You move from victim to hero, from survival to arrival.

Triggers form as we become numb and/or accustom to what is happening and someone tells us we should change. There was even a time, in my life, where I was triggered by certain words, and I would react badly. One of them was the word "unhealthy." I still do not like the word, but I am able to discuss it. I do not know if what I went through and the things I did were unhealthy. In retrospect, they may have been the healthiest things I could have done because it got me to where I am today, but did I need to go through it? That is a different question.

I would say some things I did were not good choices. They were not things I would choose for anyone else because they could have led to disastrous outcomes, but for me, they ultimately led to freedom.

One way to know that you are healed is when you become neutral to the things that used to trigger you. When someone said "Unhealthy" to me, I would have said that they were judging me. Now, I know differently.

What Does Life Look Like When You Are Free?

When I gave my skeletons names, they no longer controlled my life. I stepped into my authentic skin and became empowered by the amazing feeling of freedom to be who I was created to be. I am no longer influenced by the voices of society and others who tell me what I should do, how I should look, and what I should or should not say. I do not give a rip anymore because I am happy in my own skin.

I recognize my purpose now and am empowered by a dream that started at the age of seventeen, which is to help others connect with their true self, let go of the past, and create a life of abundant joy. I wish I could tell you that the skeletons are gone, but that would be a lie. They are still there and every once in while one of them pops up their head and speaks to me. I call them by name and have learned to listen to them.

When I try to hide or bury them, they have power in my life, and I tend to act reactively. When I listen, I hear those old patterns and false stories calling my name. Knowing them by name allows me to listen differently, create a positive narrative, and live life out loud.

This book is about learning to recognize those skeletons, how they speak to you, and how to name them. The first part of this book is my story of a lifetime of abuse, shame, guilt, PTSD, and drugs. You will be amazed at how much I have gone through in life and survived. I joke that I am a cat with nine lives because I have come close to death so many times, yet God had a different plan for me.

The second part is how I got free and how you can too. I share with you the tools that I wish someone would have given me. I show you that there is hope, no matter what you have been through. Resilience was what led to new life repeatedly. That resilience comes from the ability to review, rewrite, and retell the story. If I can go through what I have been and have it turn out good, then you can change your life as well.

It is time for you to be free, to get unstuck. Are you ready? This is a journey that you will never regret taking. Will it be hard at times? Will there be times when you go back to those familiar patterns? Maybe. However, if you do not quit and keep moving forward, I promise you this: life will get better.

The only time to start is now. Let's turn the page and get started.

Chapter 1:

My First Skeleton–The Outsider

It's okay to fight for someone who loves you. It's not okay to fight for someone to love you. That's a huge difference.

Unknown

For as long as I can remember, I felt like an outsider, like I did not belong. I looked different, thought different, and was super sensitive to outside stimulation. Some of my earliest memories include learning that I was not planned, which I assigned to the "not wanted" category. Then, later in my preteen years, I remember my mom telling me she should have aborted me. Feeling like an outsider, both in my family and in the general public, laid the foundation for what would become

15

a progressive downward spiral in my life until I hit my last, rock bottom.

Abandonment, both emotional and physical, is something no child should ever experience or feel, and yet my childhood was filled with it. I never felt accepted for who I was. Instead, I was made to feel like I was a burden, the unwanted one.

From a young age, I could tell that I was different from my family, but not only did I feel different, I also looked different from them. Looking and acting differently even included my extended family and my grandparents on both my maternal and paternal sides. When we were together and everyone would be talking and enjoying themselves, I almost always felt alone and rejected.

Sometime around the age of nine, I determined that the reason I felt the way I did about not belonging to my family was my conclusion that my dad was not my real dad! I was sure that was the answer. When I told my parents that I figured out that mom was pregnant with me before they got married, she acknowledged that. Then I became quite vocal and insisted that my dad was not my biological father. They both denied it, but in my heart, I knew the truth. That introduced another aspect of me feeling like an outsider: betrayal. I could not understand why they would not tell me the truth and I was going to hound them until they told me.

It was not long after my revelation that they'd had enough of my banter and sent me to a shrink, Dr. Plotkin. Talk about feeling betrayed. I knew I was right, and my parents thought there was something seriously wrong with me! I had several sessions with him, and then he had a meeting with all of us and told my parents that I was not crazy. Instead, he suggested the problem was with them and that I had an extremely high IQ.

That explained a lot. From the time I was little, I got bored easily and I was naturally curious; I always wanted more information. Mom said I never wanted to take naps because I did not want to miss anything in life.

I guess my need for knowledge started before I could speak. By the time I was eighteen months old, I was able to talk in full sentences. According to the notes my parents kept in my baby book, it was shortly thereafter that I had my first argument. Daddy had put me to bed, and I asked him to keep the light on. He told me that I could not have my bedroom light on because the light was on in the kitchen and that was enough. Apparently, I disagreed, and I replied, "I'm not sleeping in the kitchen."

After my final session with Dr. Plotkin, I hoped that things would be different, that maybe now I would be seen for who I really was and that they would accept me, but that did not happen. Everything stayed the same. As a matter of fact, I felt like the punishment for things that I was not responsible for got worse. The exaggerated and painful spanking increased.

The feeling of abandonment became real in my life the moment my younger sister was born. By the time she was three years old, she became the star of the family. Everybody *loved* her, showered her with affection and attention, and, occasionally, tolerated me. It got to the point that if she did something wrong, I was the one who got punished for it and not just a little bit.

Recently, I saw my mom and we were reminiscing about the past because my husband shared a picture of a paddle his parents had in their kitchen. It made him feel nostalgic. I asked if he ever got spanked with it, and my mom interrupted and very cavalierly said, "Oh, well, we used to hit Shari with a breadboard." I was sitting there, and I literally choked on my water. Then I said, "I would not call it spanking. Dad hit me with a breadboard up to 30 times in a row, regularly." She denied it; of course, my memory was wrong yet again. "What is wrong with you, mom?" I asked. How can she not remember the brutality? I do not know if it is funny or tragic how some people do not remember the bad things they did, even when others remind them. My guess is that there is a built-in protection; we tell ourselves stories to make life a bit easier to survive.

There was also little stability in my life because we moved every two years and not only within the same city or school district. Instead, we moved around the country from state to state. We always moved in July or August just before the school year started. In every new school I was the outsider, desperately trying to fit in, and just as I really made friends and started to feel like I belonged, we moved again. I was never able to form that solid bond with others, where you learned to just be okay with your differences, because I barely got to know somebody.

Each time we moved, I felt more abandoned and betrayed by the people that were making these decisions: my parents. As I look back, I realize that those feelings of being an outsider created skeletons that formed a deep desire for acceptance and love that would later lead me down some destructive paths. I am so thankful that the Lord spared my life, time and time again.

The abandonment that left the biggest scar and brought the outlier skeleton out of the closet came when I was just seventeen years old. I learned, while away with a friend on vacation, that our house was sold and that my mother's boyfriend asked her and my sister to move in with him. The decision was made, and my mother called me to say that she and my fifteen-year-old sister would be moving in with him and that I would have to make other arrangements. My mother's decision reinforced the feeling that I was not wanted and that I simply did not matter. I will be sharing more about that story and the effect it had on my life later in this book.

Some Light in the Dark Places

·I did not feel safe or trust most people I knew, but there were two people who brought light into my life and planted seeds that are now coming to fruition. My fourth-grade teacher, Mr. McCloud, showed me how to believe in myself. He went out of his way to make me feel like I belonged. He satisfied my quest for knowledge, and even invited the class over to make ice cream at his house and go swimming in his pool. Today, that would be creepy, and he would be suspected to be a child molester, but it was very normal back then. He was the one who said to me, "You know what Shari? You're a leader." That was the first time I had ever heard someone refer to me as a leader. He encouraged me to push harder with my schoolwork, embraced my creativity, and inspired me to be a school safety.

I became an after-school crossing guard with a sash and shield. I felt like I made a difference. I got to help people cross the street safely after school to make it home. It was the first time I remember feeling like I had a purpose and was smart. What's interesting is that I was nine years old, which was the same time my parents were making me doubt myself and question my sanity and intuition.

The second person who I remember made a big difference came into my life after my parents got separated the first time, and just before I turned twelve. He was my mother's new boyfriend, Bert, and it was a wonderful thing. He loved me as if I were his own daughter.

This man showed interest in me, he interacted with me as if I mattered, and he listened to me. I felt unconditional love from a grown man for the first time ever, but it also contained a dagger. A year into the relationship, he asked my mom to marry him and she listened to the voices in her head that told her she should really try to work it out with my dad. I was heartbroken.

My parents got back together and a few weeks later, just before I was to start high school, we moved from Maryland to California. At the same time, Bert moved back to California and rekindled his marriage and family. What I thought was a gift, an anchor, became yet another adult who abandoned me. Fast forward to today: the man I loved so dearly as a preteen is in my life once again, but I don't have the relationship I had with him back then. It saddens me; I've never had that experience with another man as a father figure. Don't get me wrong, I am loved by my father and my stepfather, but those relationships have not always felt unconditional or supportive.

As the skeletons enter our life and create a home in the closets of our minds, we develop survival skills to live with them. Over the years, I have had so many skeletons take up space; some of them were good, but unfortunately most were not. The older I got, the less I was able to recognize and understand them and the feelings accompanying them, and the more unwise choices I made.

As a child, one of my ways to hide and retreat was with books and reading. It gave me a reprieve from the world. I would immerse myself in fiction. Imagination is a powerful thing. When I found books that I identified with the story, I would read and commit them to memory. That way, I could transport myself into the character and/or place and live vicariously.

The abandonment issues I developed in my childhood followed me into adulthood. The fear of abandonment shows up in many different ways. One thing is for certain: it leaves you hungry for love and acceptance. There are times in my adult life that I sacrificed myself and turned my back on my own needs because my desire to be wanted was more important than anything else. I allowed boys and men to treat me badly, take advantage of me, and abuse me all because I never learned what real love was supposed to be. When adults that are supposed to love you abandon you, it is natural to choose partners and friends that are emotionally unavailable or leave you feeling abandoned.

If you recognize yourself in this chapter of my story, then understand that abandonment feelings can appear in subtle ways. Sometimes, we allow others to mistreat us, and other times we abandon ourselves.

It becomes a vicious cycle that you feel you cannot get out of, but there is hope. Later in this book, I share my journey of healing and the path to forgiveness of myself and others. Don't give up. Please do not ignore your needs. I promise that it can and does get better.

Shari Lueck

Chapter 2:

Bullies

Sticks and stones may break my bones, but names will never hurt me.

Old Adage

I wish that saying was true, but words do hurt and sometimes the words cut so deep that the wounds they create cannot be stitched together. These wounds can cause pain long after broken bones and bruises heal. Name-calling and hurtful language often become the skeleton's backbone or framework for how we perceive ourselves.

The Bible says that "Death and life are in the power of the tongue, and those who love it will eat its fruit." Our words have power to build or to destroy. Throughout my life, words have been used as daggers to destroy my sense of self and have derailed my self-esteem. My early life was filled with language used to knock me down.

As I write about the times in my younger years, I find it important to note that my childhood was filled with a lot of good moments and memories too. I am confident that I was loved and that my parents' intention was always good. However, when we do not take the time to learn from our own pain and purposely make changes, our best is sometimes hurtful to others.

Home was not always a safe place for me. I never felt the sense of peace or ease that home is considered to bring. For as far back as I can remember, nothing I ever did was good enough. Crying without a visible reason, like bleeding or a broken bone, was not tolerated. I learned that showing or sharing emotion was not okay for me.

As part of Generation X, I was a latch key kid from the time I was in second grade. There was nobody home to make me a snack or discuss the day with. Instead, I was expected to come home, do my homework, and then play outdoors until the streetlights came on.

When I was seven, one day after school, I took my mom's bike to go play. My purple Schwinn had been stolen the week before. Mom's bike was too big for me, but if I stood up while I rode, I could manage it just fine. The only challenge was stopping; I did not know how to use the handbrakes. I was going down a very steep hill that formed a "T" at the bottom. Well, that is how I knew that the handbrakes were a challenge for me. As I picked up speed from the downhill force, I could not use the brakes to slow down and, yep, you guessed it, I crashed. The bicycle hit the curb at full speed, the front tire bent in half, and I flew over the handlebars like Evil Knievel, dragging my face along the sidewalk, using my bare knees as brakes.

I remember the incident like it was yesterday. I also remember getting into trouble for riding my mother's bike. Accidents are not called "on purpose" for a reason. My welfare was never discussed, only the damage to the bicycle. Words were used like "reckless", "selfish", "careless", and "rude" when addressing what happened. I was none of those things.

As the years rolled past, I was called names by those that were supposed to protect me, and I was blamed for things I did not do, especially where my sister was involved. I did not know why she could do no wrong, but if something happened, it was my fault.

My younger sister bullied me, and not just verbally. She called me names, but she liked to hit me, and hiding behind a bedroom door led to holes being kicked into the door. It seemed like she could call me whatever she wanted, break things, or hit me, but if I even tried to defend myself, I would get in trouble for being mean to my sister.

This one time stands out in my mind and left scars on my body. She and I were home alone one weekday afternoon. We were both young teens. She got really, really mad at something I said and started to take it out on me physically. I could not get away from her. Then, finally, after we got close enough to the front door, I was able to shove her outside of the house and lock the door.

That proved to be an awfully bad decision, but at the time, it was the best solution to end her tirade. Man, was I ever wrong. The next thing I knew she had punched the glass in the windowpane on the door with her fist and I found myself standing there on the other side with two, big glass pieces sticking out from where they pierced my neck.

There was hell to pay when my parents came home from work that day. I had what looked like a vampire bite on my neck and the front door had only remnants of glass left in the frame.

Of course, it was all my fault. I was the one that locked my sister out and her rage was justified. Once again, it was them against me. Bullying in my home was sometimes covert, but it still hurt, nonetheless.

No Place Was Safe

I was in the second grade, walking home from school one day by myself because no one else would walk with me. We lived in Chapel Hill, North Carolina at the time and I remember wearing my Brownie uniform. I heard a group of kids off in the background but turned around and saw nothing. The next thing I knew, they were not far behind me and we were scuffling. One of the kids hit my head with a rock just behind my right ear. The pain was searing, and my head started gushing. I could not believe what happened. I was standing there with my hand filling with blood, scared of what might happen next. Fortunately, when they that saw I was hurt, they ran.

Two years later, I was nine years old and new to another neighborhood and elementary school. Every day when I walked home from school, I turned onto Eastridge Lane, the street we lived on, and one of the neighbors, Gwen, would come out, chase me home, and smash me down on the steps leading up to the front door of my house. I would tell my parents, but for weeks they did nothing to protect me. One day, they must have gotten fed up with my complaining and finally did something. My mother went over to talk to Gwen's parents. Then, the next day, instead of Gwen coming out, her brother started shooting his BB gun at me out of the second-story window of their house when I walked by.

What really hurt was that the ones who were supposed to love me the most saw what was happening and did nothing. It was bad enough that they bullied me, I could accept that, but the fact that they did not protect me from others created a deep wound in my heart. It signified that I was not worthy of anything, that I deserved to be treated worse than a rodent.

In addition to physical altercations, over the years, there was a lot of name-calling from kids at school and people at home. When I was a teen, my stepfather had a cousin who called me "harelip" every time he saw me. To this day, my parents laugh about that. Why wouldn't they stop it?

Bullying had a profound effect on my life and set in motion a pattern of thought and absent boundaries that taught me name-calling or shoving me around was acceptable behavior, and that I deserved anything I got in life. Once that mindset sticks, it is hard to change. I was divided. There was a big part of me that believed I deserved to be treated poorly, but there was always a tiny voice inside that said I deserved better and I would fight back.

As I got older and grew up into an adult, being mistreated was something I was used to and expected; I normalized it. It seemed I was always waiting for someone to show their true colors and hurt me. I never learned boundaries or how to respect myself. If the people who were supposed to love me treated me this way, then I believed something was wrong with me.

The pain was so bad at times that I had suicidal thoughts and fantasies about disappearing. I would joke that my real parents would come and get me because, like adopted kids, I would be wanted. I will talk more about that later in the book.

For years, I did not know what gave me the resilience I had. I did not recognize where my strength came from or the ability to get back up and stand a little taller after each fall. I used to joke that God must have big plans for me because I have been tested and survived more times than most people have in an entire lifetime.

Today, I believe that we are given lessons until we learn what we need to learn so we can help others. That is one of the reasons why I wrote this book. I am passionate and on fire with a mission to help others, and I'm committed to my purpose.

I know who I am and who I was created to be. I love myself and I love others. The funny thing is now that I am in this place where the skeleton, who used to remind me that I am not loveable, no longer has power in my life, I see there are many people who truly love me for exactly who I am.

I have had many friends throughout life. Some for a season, some for a reason, and some for a lifetime. Some of those friends disappeared for years on end and resurfaced again. Others left for good. As I sit here writing, there are a handful of friends that are different from all others.

Shortly after I had moved to Orlando, eight years ago, I met someone. She was distant and cold to me as an "outsider", yet she had a smile and a laugh that could light up a room. It was obvious she was an anchor to a small group of like-minded individuals. One evening, after a meeting where this group gathered, the lady with the smile and confidence I admired asked me if I'd like to go to Starbucks and get some tea or coffee with her and a couple of friends. I do not know why I said yes, but I did not hesitate. That night literally changed my life. Vicki and I became fast friends. We had a bond that to this day cannot be severed by time or distance, by anger or disappointment, or by voids of interaction. I have a friend in her like I never imagined.

Vicki Sanner, my BFF, and soul sister suggested I participate in an intensive coaching program facilitated by Charlene Sears, that opened the closet hiding all my skeletons and put them out on parade for me to get to know intimately. The group watched me confront and then release my blame and shame. That weekend cracked me open and created the badass woman I am today: vulnerable, transparent, empathetic, and courageous. She is truly a gift that I will forever treasure.

A job promotion led me from Orlando back to my hometown just north of Los Angeles. Feeling heartbroken after leaving the best friend I have ever had; I was reconnected with someone I barely knew ten years earlier. That person is now my husband.

Tommy is the definition of what I always thought a man was supposed to be. He is kind, compassionate, loving, and strong. We built our friendship by hiking together. Neither of us were interested in anything other than friendship, and what a friendship we developed. Tommy showed me what unconditional love looked and felt like.

When someone thinks "this is the one" because they make you feel alive, nervous, and apprehensive, I would challenge that. Love does not hurt. Love does not make you wonder. Love is safe. Love is the calm in the storm.

Love lifts you up when you are down and sits beside you when you are scared. There are no secrets and no fears. If I could, I would give back time to Tommy, so we'd have more time together.

I also have newer, yet amazing friends that I have met along my journey. A newer friend, Tammy Collins, encouraged me to follow my dream and write this book. She made me believe that my story needed to be shared and has the power to change lives.

Sometimes the Skeletons Try to Sneak Back In

As I am writing this, the United States is in conflict and upheaval. Here we are, three months into a global pandemic, dealing with the novel coronavirus, and the murder of George Floyd, murdered by the police, has brought systemic racism and equality to the forefront. The people are tired of institutional racism and not feeling safe from those hired to protect them.

Seeing the video of George's murder took me to a place I have not been and brought back feelings that I have not felt in a very long time. It stirred deep and uncomfortable feelings inside of me, and I realized that powerful bully skeleton was trying to get back in. I felt full of fear and outrage. I did not feel safe and was worried about all my loved ones. I did not want to leave my house, but as I worked through my fear, I realized those feelings were coming from that place in my heart that had been scarred long ago.

I talked to a friend about the turmoil I felt inside, and she reminded me of one very important thing: I am never alone and have nothing to fear. My faith is stronger than my fear. I know that God has preserved my life so many times that I am not leaving this earth one minute before my time. So, instead of shrinking and allowing fear to hold me down one more time, I decided to get loud and stare it in the face. Nobody is ever going to bully me again.

Maybe you have allowed others to bully you and/or not treat you properly with the respect you deserve. Have you allowed fear to keep you trapped? Have you stayed silent to stay out of harm's way? Chances are, you are like me and, in your closet, there is a skeleton that needs to be faced. Towards the end of this book, I am going spell out exactly what I did to heal, but right now I want to give you some hope.

If you have people at home, at work, or in your social life that bully you, now is a good time to think about your boundaries. Think about boundaries as aid, not borders or blockades. Boundaries are put in place to respect our needs and wants, and then used to ask others to respect them too.

Tune into your feelings. Is there something you need, but have not verbalized? What do you want and/or need?

There is hope even in the darkest places, and I want to encourage you to honor yourself and believe that you really do have what it takes to create the life you want. When we find ourselves in a story, we do not like nor belong in, we have the power to rewrite it. I will teach you how. It is worth it, and you can start right now.

Chapter 3:

Turning Fear Into Power

Courage is resistance to fear, mastery of fear, not absence of fear.

Mark Twain

F ear is a complex and powerful emotion. It is so complicated you may not even realize you are experiencing or expressing it. Often when you are bold and make powerful statements like, "I am not afraid of anything," you are telling the world that you are scared. We all are afraid of something and feeling fear is a normal emotion.

The truth is, for most of us, fear is present on a regular basis, but the form that it chooses to present itself in is constantly changing. Maybe you experience anxiety, a deep nervousness, confusion, lack of motivation, uncertainty, or something unidentifiable deep within.

Chances are, you're experiencing fear on a magnitude of levels and in multiple forms all at once. Fear can be sneaky like that! It always shows up in disguise to try to trick you.

From the time I was a young child, fear played a significant role in my life. You have already read about my encounters with bullies, both in school and within my family. Even though I left those bullies behind, the words and fears I attached to them followed me on my journey into adulthood. Fear forms a central theme in this book.

The key to coping with fear is learning you can be both brave and afraid. Your fears do not define you. Fear is a natural emotion and reaction that connects to your sense of survival, but it does not have to be a bad thing. Fear can also be a positive force that empowers you because it shows the areas you need to grow in.

Everyone on this planet experiences fear but what sets successful and happy people apart from everyone else is their ability to act in the face of fear. Now you might be wondering, "How do I know if I am experiencing fear and what do I do with this feeling, regardless of whether it's fear or not?" The answer is simple. **Know that where there's fear, there's power.**

Fear Is Within Us All

Fear is a vital response to physical and emotional danger that has been pivotal throughout evolution. If people did not feel fear, they would not be able to protect themselves from legitimate threats.

Although public speaking, elevators, and spiders generally do not present immediate, dire consequences, some people still develop extreme fight, flight, or freeze responses to specific objects or scenarios.

Everyone experiences occasional bouts of fear, such as when giving a high-stakes presentation, or feelings of "nerves," such as going on a first date. When a fear is persistent, specific to a certain threat, and impairs your life or growth, you might develop a phobia where even imagined threats feel real and you react to it.

Over time, you build walls to avoid the perceived danger. Sometimes the most seemingly harmless things can become a source of fear.

For example, you may be afraid of clowns because you secretly watched *It* as a child after your parents went to sleep. Now, every time you see a clown, you panic in fear because you have developed coulrophobia. Fear of clowns is a relatively common fear, but this type of phobic, fearful reaction can be triggered by anything you have developed a negative association with.

Fears affect how you regulate yourself. In a fearful situation, you get an unknown worry, but you may not have the ability to identify the specific trigger that sets it off. Therefore, you cannot remove yourself from the situation and escape the fear of that impending threat. All you can do is experience that unsafe and unsettled feeling.

When you are fearful, you put up barriers where they do not need to be; however, at the same time, you also knock down barriers in some places where you need protection. This can throw off your safety barometer.

It has taken time and a lot of practice, but I have learned to become aware of how I feel when I notice that I am afraid or unsettled. I can identify the trigger that allows me to decide if the fear is real and whether I need to either pay attention to it or let it go. Fear no longer paralyzes me, but it is a warning sign that tells me there is something wrong I need to deal with. It has become a powerful tool in my life for looking inward and seeing where healing needs to take place.

Sometimes the fear is real, and I need to put healthy boundaries in place. Sometimes the fear is a conditioned response from my past that has been triggered and I need to go through the process of letting it go.

How Do You Respond to Fear?

People often think of fear as a negative emotion. However, fear has a function: to reduce harm and keep you safe. Fear has the ability to save your life because your body tells you that you are in danger and can react accordingly. This is known as the fight-or-flight response. If a car is barreling down the street directly toward you, your instinct will likely be to jump out of the way.

However, there is another response to fear that is not typically thought about: freezing. Fear has the power to immobilize you in the face of danger. When that car comes barreling toward you, there is a chance you may not jump out of the way and might stay frozen in fear.

My own response to fear is evident in many different ways.

When Dreams Become Nightmares

For me, fear became an emotion to avoid at all costs. I numbed myself to fear and ended up in extremely dangerous life-threatening situations because of that.

Looking back, from the age of four, I never felt safe. Fear lived in the forefront of my mind, even in good moments when there was absolutely nothing to be afraid of. I could not enjoy those good moments because I knew that they were fleeting and soon something bad was going to happen.

For ten years, starting around age three, I suffered daily from severe nightmares. Most of the time, they would happen in a sequence, and they were so vivid I can still remember them as clear as day.

In the first nightmare, a very tall, slender man would approach me as I slept in my bedroom. This man was dressed in loosely draped clothing, with red pants, a green top, a white, pointy pompom-like hat, and long, straight, white pointy shoes–like an elf from the dark underbelly of the North Pole.

As he approached me, he would hold out his arms, which were shaped like forklifts. He would slide those forklift arms under my body and lift me out of bed, my body becoming as stiff as a plank. While he carried me, my body would rotate but his elbows would never move. Turning, he would walk me out to the hall and lift me up to a long, fluorescent tube light on the hall ceiling that burned me.

No matter where I lived, it was always the same fluorescent hallway light, which I do not recall existing in any house I had lived in, and I had lived in many homes throughout my childhood.

In the second nightmare, tiny thumb-sized men lived in a secret village under my bed. This village was full of hundreds of tiny men, who largely resembled the characters in *The Borrowers* but dressed like the dwarves in *Snow White*. These tiny men had one mission: to build a fire that would spark and set my bed on fire, burning me to death.

The last nightmare, which I have also experienced in adulthood, usually happened after I had been excessively spanked as a child. This nightmare involved tires, complete with hubcaps and rims. The tires would whirl around in the air like a cyclone, hurling in different directions and at me. In the dream, I would have to dodge them to avoid getting hit.

As an adult, people have offered to analyze these dreams for me, but I always say no. If God wants me to face these things, He will bring it up to me and put it in front of my face to see. For now, my focus is to rewrite the story of my past and turn it into something that will fuel the fire for the powerful soul I am today.

Living Through Fear

There are three main elements that come up when I talk about the experience of fear: intensity, timing, and coping.

Intensity comes with the severity of the threat. The bigger the threat to your safety, the bigger your fear will be. When you are younger and get caught doing something bad, you might get spanked or punished and think to yourself, "Well, that is going to hurt but I will survive." When things become more intense, you start to build up a tolerance and become more careless.

Timing also greatly affects how you process fear. If the fear is immediate, you have a much stronger reaction than if the fear could happen in the future. If it becomes a "maybe fear," you become more relaxed about it. However, this can cause you to miss the fears immediately in front of you when you are looking at the bigger picture down the road.

Some people tell me, "Shari, you went from surviving to thriving." To me, you must arrive before you can thrive. People who survive tend to repress their emotions and turn off their fears to numb themselves. What you need to do is get grounded, learn to recognize those emotions, and learn how to let them help you.

Next comes coping, which involves stepping back and looking at the situation to validate the fear and see how you can either handle this threat or eliminate it. When you know which steps you can take to eliminate the threat, you can overcome or move through your fear. However, when you feel helpless, you cannot control that fear and it intensifies. That is when you build up those high levels of panic and terror.

It is certain that fear can be a drag, and there are situations and life-threatening circumstances that stir up a whole new kind of fear that I would never wish for anyone. But there's another spectrum of fear that comes from within and the culprit is often our very own "lizard brain" and feelings of self-worth. Most likely, it's this very fear that is holding you back from living the wildly successful, abundant, joy-filled life that you crave and deserve.

Fear has tried to take hold of me several times recently. The biggest fear I have faced recently coincided with the decision to write this book and occasionally stills rears its ugly head. I decided to take the entrepreneurial plunge and hung up my 9-5 hat as an executive in Corporate America just before the pandemic knocked us all off our feet.

My relationship with my personal forms of fear took on a new set of definitions. I think anytime we face the unknown, fear tries to stop us, but this actually surprised me. I was fearful that I wasn't smart enough to write a book, never mind start a new business. I was afraid that people would think I was stupid or not experienced enough to prove that I know what I am talking about. Never mind the set of fears surrounding the belief that nobody would want to listen to anything I have to say.

The list of crazy thoughts and irrational fears that surfaced for me when I started this adventure are endless. And guess what? I now realize that they are just thoughts based around old limiting beliefs, and they are not true. My thoughts do not define me, and my fears are lies of my own making.

The truth is, for most of us, fear is present on a regular basis, but the form that it chooses to present itself in is constantly changing. Maybe you experience anxiety, a deep nervousness, confusion, lack of motivation, uncertainty, or something unidentifiable deep within. Whatever they may be, you can change them. (Lawrence Robinson and Melinda Smith)

Turn Your Skeletons Into POWER

> *"Do one thing every day that scares you."*

> *Eleanor Roosevelt*

Everything I have gone through with hiding from and avoiding fear has helped shape the person I am today. It has given me the ability to help others through their fear with compassion and respect. While I know I am highly intuitive and an empath, I have developed an ability to help other people cope with their fear responses without absorbing their fears. I will go to great lengths to help someone else feel safe, even if it means sacrificing my own safety to do so.

I mentioned in the last chapter that I am writing this book at a time when there is significant turmoil in the United States. After seeing the video of George Floyd's murder, I started to feel a paralyzing fear try to come over me. Seeing the racial tensions boiling up within the country has triggered intense memories and emotions inside me. I began to feel those unsafe and panicky feelings that caused my PTSD twenty-one years ago as I was watching circumstances around me, I cannot control become more volatile. Immediately, I recognized those panicky feelings as fear.

47

To overcome that fear, I had to get to the root of the problem and identify where that fear was coming from. This meant diving in and educating myself on the situation in the world around me. I started listening, reading, and learning about how racism is perpetuated and why it is not enough to be "non-racist." This took away my fear and helped me face the fact that, even though those feelings of fear come, I can get past it and fight for others who are afraid and cannot fight for their own safety.

I will not live in fear anymore. Fear-driven behaviors prevent us from being resilient and standing up when we see things that are not right and need to be fixed. They are very real, and prevalent in daily life and society.

Fear is a dynamic emotion. It can be transformed into resilience, and that resilience comes when you take things that scare you deep inside your soul and set them on fire.

The key to my resilience has been recognizing I can be a voice for myself and for others. I have developed the ability to turn my fear into vulnerability, leading to power, and you can too. However, to be a voice for others, you need to be a voice for yourself first.

In the past, I would always be willing to be a voice for others, but it would be at my own expense because I did not value myself. It came down to a "hurt me, not them" attitude. Now, I have learned to value myself first and it is okay to speak out when I am not being treated respectfully.

Meet yourself where you are today. Do not consider who you want to be in the future, but who you are now and how you are going to use your fear to empower yourself. Sometimes that means talking to a medical professional to help you through severe trauma. Other times that might mean turning to God (or whatever higher power you believe in) or finding a good development coach to help you uncover and embrace your inner power.

As you become more aligned with who you are and what you want in life, it gets easier to pursue your dreams with each step you take. Turning your fear into power might seem unachievable at first, but once you learn how to use the power you have right now to change your future. It can be done; I am living proof of that!

Here are some simple steps that I take to pursue my personal passions and ideas, despite fear that often creeps in.

Make time to focus on self-reflection and positive self-talk.

Next time you feel nervous, anxious, afraid, or uncertain, dig deep and look what's really buried underneath those feelings. Are you nervous to apply for that job because you're afraid of rejection? What if you don't get the job? Does that mean you're not good enough and that you'll never experience the career success you long for?

Of course, this isn't true, but it's all too common to participate in that negative and harmful self-talk. In most cases, somewhere deep, you've created a limiting belief that reminds you that you're not worthy to experience happiness or success. Be honest with yourself and identify what's at the root of your fear. (Lawrence Robinson)

Now take that negative statement and write an empowering statement that's the opposite of your limiting belief. For example, if your limiting belief is "I don't deserve to experience true success because I haven't worked hard enough," flip it and write "I deserve to experience success on my own terms, all while having fun and living in abundance along the way!"

Next, weigh your Options.

Ask yourself what the payoff is. Then, make a list of pros and cons of what would happen if:

You pursued your passions and vision, despite your fear or you choose to maintain status quo

I'm guessing that you will realize that there are a lot more pros to act in the face of fear than there are to maintain status quo.

Now it is time to Act.

You have the tools and can act in the face of fear without your whole world crashing down on you. All you have to do, is actually DO IT! Take that very first step in the positive direction. The first step is often the hardest. Remember to take one step at a time.

Remember, you are changing patterns and removing your limiting beliefs. Be kind and patient with yourself and the process you're going through.

Celebrate You

Take time to acknowledge yourself for facing your fears and celebrate your successes, no matter how big or small, along the way. This will feed your positive momentum and will reinforce the process.

Each time you choose to look beneath the surface and uncover what's truly behind your fear, you step forward and closer to reclaiming your personal power. (Kallal)

Chapter 4:

Darkness

*As far as we can discern, the sole purpose of human existence is to
kindle a light in the darkness of mere being.*

Carl Jung

Recently, I went on a trip to Fantastic Caverns in
Springfield, Missouri. During the tour, we
learned that his was the first natural cave in
North America to get electricity. While we were there, our
tour stopped in the middle of the cave and turned off all
light sources – even our watches and cell phones had to be
disabled. We were standing in pure darkness, surrounded
by what felt like emptiness.

Back in the 1800s, when the cave was discovered, they
did not have cell phones or watches, or even flashlights.
They had candlelight and the Edison light bulb. Once our

guide turned these on to show us what the original explorers would have seen, we were able to examine the cave with a little spotlight the way they would have done 200 years ago. Suddenly, we could see the walls and corridors.

This experience made me think about the darkness I have faced in my life. When you are standing in true darkness, there is no light, no reflection to allow sight. Did you know your eyes can only see when there is some form of light to guide you?

I used to think that darkness was pure pain. In hindsight, I have come to understand that, for me, darkness is the experience of many emotions. It is the combination of feelings intertwined and overwhelming. Sometimes, darkness for me also feels like a void.

Throughout my life, and well into my 40s, I lived in and out of darkness. Instead of understanding and dealing with my feelings, I pushed through and ignored them, or ran. Rarely did I stop to think about what I was experiencing or how I felt. Nor did I consider how my decisions might impact my future, or even the next choice I would make along the way.

So as we find ourselves, from time to time, in a dark space, we might start by recognizing it, then checking on it to make sure it is safe for us, and if it is, we could then allow it. *Just sad tonight. Feeling blue. Disconnected. Grieving. Confused. Anxiety creeping in a bit. Had a fight. Lost my wallet. Bored with my job. Tired. Hungry. Achy. Angry.* Everybody ends up in these places. If we find ourselves in these darkened places, we can fight against them—and sometimes we should— but we can also breathe into them, relax our bodies and feelings, have a good cry or a short pity party. We don't have to run or fight. (Eleanor Haley)

When the tide washes in on the shore, it comes in quickly, rolls back out slowly, and then returns in another wave. Darkness comes in waves in this same way.

Crying Out for Help in the Darkness

My first real cry for help came when I was 18 years old. I had found myself homeless for the second time in my life. While I was away, my roommate stole everything I owned, racked up a $900 long distance phone bill (yes, we used to pay for phone calls), and disappeared. Everything was gone – my clothes, shoes, furniture, car radio, and even my silverware.

Riddled with debt, a pile of bills, and only the items I had brought with me on the trip, I was devastated and did not know what to do. I asked my mom for help and guidance. She offered to pay the utility bills, and then said,

"I don't know what to tell you, Shari. Maybe your grandparents in Pennsylvania will take you in."

This really hurt me. My dad was not in my life at the time, and my mother lived right here with my sister. Why should I have to go all the way to Pennsylvania to live with my grandparents? Moving in with my mom, even temporarily was clearly not an option.

With no other choice, I packed up what little I had and went to live with my maternal grandparents in Erie, Pennsylvania. Both my grandparents were sedentary and acted elderly. They certainly did not live a lifestyle healthy for a young, 18-year-old adult. My grandfather had become an angry alcoholic and rarely engaged in any pleasantries. Grandma was resigned to life as it now was. They also had cats, and I am deathly allergic to cats.

I felt alone and abandoned again, and I could not see a way out. So, I set out to find a job at a local department store so I could earn some money and develop a plan. I believed my life was not worth living.

Not long after I moved, I woke up at 4AM in excruciating pain and ended up in the hospital. I spent a week there undergoing tests, feeling alone, sick, and terrified. At the time, I was told that all the tests were inconclusive, and the only diagnosis given was that my symptoms were psychosomatic. There is no way that it was psychosomatic, but this is what the doctors insisted. I later learned that it was not all in my head as suggested, but I had a ruptured ovarian cyst that became infected in my pelvis.

When I got home from the hospital, I just wanted out. I wanted the emotional and physical pain to end. I did not want to be me anymore. Suicide felt like the only answer. That is when I took a knife from the kitchen and decided to slit my wrists.

I dragged the butcher's knife across my wrists. The sensation alone was scary, but I pressed harder until I drew blood. The cuts were only one inch long and horizontal from my wrist to my elbow. They were not deep enough to kill me or even require stitches. Yet they hurt enough to stop me, and the scars are still there to remind me. At the time, I just wanted the pain to stop. I thought dying was my only way out. It is obvious now that I did not really want to die.

After that incident, I called my mom in tears and told her what I did. She told me, "You can't even do that right." Let me be clear here – this was my mom's way of showing tough love. She was not telling me I should kill myself. She was trying to tell me that maybe this was a sign.

At the time, I believed that nobody loved nor cared about me. However, this time was also a blessing because I realized that I did want to live, but not the way I was living, anymore. My desire to become somebody I could be proud of took over and I went into action.

I decided to apply to college and got accepted at Penn State, the only school I applied to, and was set to start in the January semester. Penn State is where I was born, so to me everything was tying back. After I got accepted, I called my dad and told him what had happened and my plans to attend Penn State. He had no idea that I was even in Pennsylvania and was in shock after I recounted my recent experiences. He flew me out to live with him before I started school and arranged for me to see a doctor to figure out what was going on.

This man, my dad, who I believed hated me and had not been in my life, was suddenly there for me. Not just to listen but offering to help me. My father became a beacon of hope and shone a light into my darkness.

Most of the time, we think about darkness as hopelessness or as pain. When you are in the depths of despair, and feeling so much pain, it is difficult to find a shimmer of light in the darkness. Without a reflection, it is next to impossible to see a place to start.

In my experience, this is what ultimately leads some people to commit suicide. Death becomes the ultimate solution to escape from the pain. Sometimes we cannot see a way out and the darkness envelops and consumes us. Wanting to die is a way to find a kind of relief just to see light. When you cannot find a light, you have no sense of direction and feel lost, like there is no way out. You are essentially stuck in a pit, and every time you turn, you hit another wall.

There is a difference between being clinically depressed and being suicidal. Not all people with depression are suicidal and not all suicide victims are depressed.

"The Woman Who Couldn't Have Kids"

After my dad helped me get out of my darkness, I was able to see the light and get the help I needed to attend to my medical needs.

When I got to my dad's house, he sent me to see a good gynecologist, who performed a laparoscopy. It turns out, unsurprisingly, I had been right all along. What I had was not, in fact, psychosomatic, but an ovarian cyst that had burst. Since it went unnoticed, it had become infected and caused a mass to grow inside my uterus. It had become so bad that the doctor gave me antibiotics to kill the infection before setting up surgery. The internal damage was so bad that it would not matter if surgery was delayed for weeks or months.

My doctor convinced me to start school as planned and come back for surgery during my summer break. Following my first college semester, my father arranged for me to fly back to Los Angeles, and I had exploratory surgery with an electroscope, and they cut me from one pelvic bone to the other. They ended up removing one tube and one ovary, but the ovary I had left was severely damaged.

What happened to me was so unusual that my case was published by Cedar-Sinai in a medical journal. They had removed this four-centimeter mass, with no indication of where it came from or how it got there, and it baffled the medical world.

My doctor informed me that if I wanted to have children later down the road, I would need to have reproductive surgery. I also had to start taking birth control pills to reduce my chances of getting cervical or uterine cancer. However, God has a way of letting us know our purpose. I would go on to have three children, all conceived while I was on the pill, with one damaged ovary. I had thought I was not supposed to have children, but clearly God meant for me to be a mother.

The Darkness Hits Back Hard

It would be a long time before all the lights would go out and I would return to total darkness. Due to circumstances beyond my control, darkness came and, like a monsoon, washed over me, nearly wiping me out. On August 10, 1999, during my middle son's fifth birthday, tragedy struck, as my children became the victims of a hate-fueled, anti-Semitic mass shooting. While they played at the North Valley Jewish Community Center, a Neo-Nazi walked in and opened fire on the children. My two oldest children were there, and while they survived, we were all traumatized and forever changed.

That man compromised my children's safety, and I began to feel the fear that comes with the absence of control and lack of safety. I did not know it at the time, but the event dimmed the fire in my soul. The embers inside me were starting to burn out. A large piece of me was lost that day and it would be the start of a long walk through hell and back.

I have a photograph of my daughter, sister, mother and me on the White House lawn with Hillary and Bill Clinton, after we participated in the Million Mom March to advocate for sensible gun laws. I was just looking at that photograph; the tears in my eyes and grief in my soul are so obvious and I still remember all those feelings vividly.

In 1999, we did not know a lot about post-traumatic stress disorder in civilians, so we lacked the tools and resources to seek proper help. At the time, we all suffered. My husband and I had gone to counselling, but it was not the right kind of counselling, and I felt that he did not understand what we were all going through. I attempted to find signs that the world was going to be okay, but I looked in the wrong places. I even insisted on moving to a different area. I obsessed over my children, lost myself in reading, working, volunteering, and whatever else I could find to give me some sense of control. It felt like I was losing all my dreams all over again, and I was spiralling downward into a pit of hell.

Soon thereafter, my husband and I separated. Then, shortly after that, I was wrongfully terminated from my job; because it was wrongful termination, my employer offered me a settlement of $10,000 per month for 12 months. I had recently purchased a house and had child support payments, so I took the settlement. While the financial aspect was appealing, I was now suffering from a loss of identity and the darkness quickly became a whole lot darker.

After I got divorced, instead of giving myself time to grieve, I moved on almost immediately and started dating other men. All I wanted was something that would make me feel seen, valuable, and desired.

I ended up in a relationship that quickly turned physically abusive. I felt embarrassed that I had found myself in this situation, but I was so terrified for my life, and my children's lives, that I did not try to end it or leave. People knew about it, including my parents, but no one tried to help me. My ex-husband would come to pick up our children and see my battered and bruised face, but he did nothing about it – not even to help his own children.

I was so embarrassed. Here I was, this strong woman who had been running a national company, making good money, leading my family, sitting on the board of directors, leading the Girl Scouts and the Cub Scouts, being the ideal modern woman. However, on the inside, I was dying. I had gone from a verbally abusive relationship to a physically abusive relationship.

With no one willing to help me, and no clue of how to help myself, I discovered that I could numb my pain with drugs. When that white powder went up my nose, I felt a false sense of light. I could not feel my pain anymore, and I was feeling creative and engaged, so I did not care that I was in danger and could end up with my jaw broken at any moment – until it happened.

This was the second time in my life that I carefully thought about suicide. I really wanted to die. I believed that everyone would be better off without me. The names I was called by my exes, the violence I was subjected to almost daily, the loss of my career, family, and home, it was all too much. I went all in and took a lot of sleeping pills, hoping to put myself to sleep and never wake up. Just like the first time, I did not actually want to die, but I wanted the pain to stop and was looking for any source of light.

God had other plans, as I woke up. When I did, I realized what a mess I had made and how bad things had become. The abuse got worse. The choking intensified. I was starting to black out from the blows to my head and the hands around my neck. I had to find a way out.

I went to court with my ex-husband to have the child support I was paying lowered since I was not working and had the children full time. The judge lowered the support, and we changed our visitations to alternating weeks, so they spent more time at their father's house. This was my way of trying to get help for myself and my kids.

Every attempt I made to not feel like myself and feel good, from the drugs to men and sex, was about trying to mask my pain. I was blind and oblivious to the ramifications and everything else that was going on around me.

I knew I had to make some changes. What had been a habit of snorting cocaine had turned into a habit of snorting meth. I read *A Million Little Pieces* by James Frey and thought if this guy could overcome his own life challenges and get off a meth addiction, I could too – so I did. It was hard. I went through about four days of extreme sickness, but I stopped doing drugs. I started to climb my way out of the darkness, and my light started getting a little brighter.

The light dimmed a little more again when my ex found me and broke into my apartment. He scaled the side of the building, climbed up the balcony, broke through the sliding glass door, and attacked me while I was in the shower. I lay there as he pinned me down, the towel he wrapped around my neck choking me, and a hammer in his hand held over my head. At one point, I opened my eyes and told him to just kill me because if he did not, we were going to fight. After I said that, we heard someone come home and he jumped back out the sliding door. I do not know if he would have killed me, but by the grace of God, my daughter had come home in time to prevent it.

My abuser continued to stalk me, even after I moved again. The next time he broke into my house, he pinned me against the bedroom wall and held a pair of scissors to my neck. Fortunately, my boyfriend had been on his way over and arrived in time to stop him. Now that I had another witness, I was able to have him arrested and worked up the courage to see that through. He ended up going to prison for two years, and while he was in prison, I finally felt free.

Feeling disconnected was always a major component of my way of dealing with my darkness. Instead of trying to seek out and name the emotions I was feeling, I looked for connection elsewhere. For a long time, I had what I call destination addiction. I believed that my next job, house, boyfriend, city, hairstyle, piece of clothing, or whatever else would hold the answer to my happiness and let the light back in.

Here is the thing about drug addiction: no one starts doing drugs because they have decided to become a drug addict. No one enters the darkness because they want to enter the darkness. We do the things we think make sense at the time. Drugs fulfill something in us that dulls the fear of the darkness. It is very scary in the dark.

Sometimes, people come out of the darkness and still have that will to live, but sometimes people do not. There is something resilient in the human spirit that keeps us going when we emerge from the darkness, but we need that crack to let the light in. Light is like our flame of life. When the flame is completely burned out, we are in trouble. However, when we can find those ashes and smoldering remains of the fire, we can build the fire again.

When we cannot find the crack of light externally, we must find it within ourselves. For some people, that crack of light might be God. For others, it might be something else. Whatever it is for you, it is important to find it.

Finding Your Light and Embracing Emotions

Emotional darkness is not always black. Sometimes, it is a dark grey, like a cold winter day that leaves you wondering when the sun will return. When I think about darkness, I think about the emotions associated with it – grief, anxiety, despair, shame, and fear.

Today's society is plagued with emotional intolerance and toxic positivity. We hear messages such as "Get over it," "Move on," or "Let go," but these messages are intolerant. Every emotion we experience is purposeful and useful, even those negative emotions. The emotions that cast the shadow of darkness over us are there to remind us to stay on our course of action and motivate us toward our goal. They are natural. Grief is there to remind us that we are connected within the web of life, and what connects us with love can also break our hearts. Fear teaches us to survive and alerts us to danger. Despair teaches us to channel our grief and repair our broken souls.

In society, however, grief is rarely tolerated, and despair or fear are even less so. We are all afraid. We all fear the vulnerability and unpredictability of our existence, but we act as though we are not. When we cannot embrace or welcome our fear, it turns into anger, substance addition or abuse, or anxiety disorders.

We do not always need to go into the darkness to find our light. Sometimes we get hangnails. They keep us caught and hold us back in these cycles of self-defeating behavior. We shame and blame ourselves. However, when we get a glimpse of what we think our lives should be, we can start to see those embers burning again and find another solution to get out.

It is never so dark that we cannot find our way out. When we stop blaming ourselves and others, we can learn to forgive. Forgiving does not mean forgetting, but when you start to forgive yourself, you can start to step forward and learn to trust yourself again.

Here are four useful things to pay attention to if we notice ourselves feeling dark

- Awareness
- Acceptance

- Discernment

- Choice

Awareness is our responsibility for knowing what we are experiencing rather than projecting it outwards, stuffing it away, or letting it leak out unconsciously.

Acceptance is the deep self-love that allows us to be okay even when we are experiencing some very uncomfortable and downright awful things.

Discernment is moving from our most mature self into an assessment of our situation. Is something needed? Can I stay in this experience? What framework do I need to put around this? Naming it as a passing emotion; seeing it as a problem to be solved; noting that there is a physical component that needs to be handled, and the like.

Choice is where we either move to a solution or allow ourselves, and this is a gift you can learn, to simply be okay with our experience.

No matter what you are going through, when you can find the source of your emotion and what is causing your darkness, you can begin to understand that it is all temporary. Feelings are temporary, and temporary feelings do not need to create a permanent end.

Shari Lueck

Chapter 5:

Abuse

Don't judge yourself by what others did to you.
C. Kennedy

L ooking back on my childhood, I am conflicted. There is a part of me that wishes I knew how to speak up about the abuse around me. I could have made it clear to any adult that listened that what was going on in my home was wrong but how could I know it was wrong? To me it was normal. Did it not happen in everyone's family?

The second part of me is grateful because it helped shape me into the person I am today. It helps me to have empathy and understanding for others who have gone through it. My pain has now become a message of healing to others and I am thankful.

According to the dictionary, there are two definitions of abuse: to use something to bad effect or for a bad purpose, or to misuse; and to treat a person or animal with cruelty or violence, especially regularly or repeatedly.

The next level, corporal punishment, refers to flogging and being punished for actions that did not require that result. I experienced both, though back then people did not talk about the line between spanking and abuse and turned a blind eye even when the line was crossed. Thankfully, today that line is clearly defined and even though the system is not perfect there is more help available to children who are being abused.

In my house, spanking, beating, and extreme abuse were normal. My dad had a very quick temper, and I was often his target. Sometimes the spankings were delivered by hand, and other times they were delivered using a breadboard, and often more than one at a time. I often wonder if he was punishing me for the fact that I was not his child.

The cycle of abuse would continue throughout my adult years, and while the abuser would change, I was always the target.

Corporal Punishment and Childhood Abuse

There are two times I can still see vividly in my mind that took place in my preteen years. Both left a mark, and I can remember every detail.

The first incident happened one day when my mother was out of town. I was sitting around our glass dining table with my father and sister. For some unknown reason, the atmosphere was heavy, and to lighten the mood I was trying to make my sister laugh. Whenever she would go to take a bite of food, or a sip of her milk, she would laugh. She was around eight years old at the time. My dad did not like what I was doing and yelled at us to stop, so we did. However, my sister could not swallow the milk she had in her mouth, and when she caught my eye, she burst out laughing and sprayed it all over the table. This led to more laughter.

In one quick move, my dad flew out of his chair so fast it fell into the wall and left a dent. He lunged at me and grabbed my arm, yanking me up from the table with so much force it moved the glass surface. After dragging me down the hallway and up 18 stairs to my bedroom, he threw me on my bed and hit me 33 times on my bottom – I know this because I counted every single blow. I tried to hold on to my sheets, but his force was too strong, and I could not hang on.

The second incident happened when I was 12 years old. My father threw a stapler at my mother from across the kitchen, and I was mad. In my mom's defense, I said some harsh words to my father, and in return, he backed me against the wall. Wrapping two hands around my neck, he lifted me off the ground a few inches. This time, I fought back. I raised my right leg and kicked him in the stomach. He let go and I ran. That was the last time my father ever laid a hand on me.

The abuse I suffered as a child would continue in various ways as I grew older. My parents moved my sister and I around the country, and eventually got divorced.

When I was 17, I came home on a Saturday afternoon to find my mom lying on the kitchen floor. Her boyfriend and my sister were both standing there, so I asked why my mom was just lying there. When no one said anything, I laughed nervously, and this turned out to be a big mistake. I was bullied out of the kitchen and down the hallway, where I was backed up against a piece of furniture and smacked around for five minutes, leaving me with bruises.

I never got an explanation or apology for that incident but feeling unwanted was familiar to me and this only amplified it. My mom tried to justify the attack, or abuse, but I stopped listening and started disassociating instead. Whenever my mom, her boyfriend, and my sister were at our house, I was out, and when they went to his house, I was not invited.

Not long after this incident, I started spending time with older boys, allowing some of them to take advantage of me because I no longer cared. At home I felt alienated and worthless, so when these boys gave me any form of attention, I welcomed it. For a few minutes at least, someone cared for me.

Feeling Helpless

When children suffer any form of abuse, they develop a deep-seated feeling of helplessness at a vulnerable age. It is confusing because the people who are supposed to be keeping you alive, who you depend on for survival, are often the ones who inflict the abuse.

After that last incident during which I fought back and my father stopped spanking me, I no longer felt helpless. Somewhere inside me, I knew that I did not deserve that treatment and found the strength to tell him, "Never again!"

A few years later when my stepfather abused me, I felt helpless again. I did not feel like anyone cared enough to stand up for me or protect me. Feeling helpless and that I was unlovable manifested in overachieving and perfectionism. The shame that accompanied my feelings told me I was not good enough and there was something seriously wrong with me.

The shame spiral is cunning. I did a good job of self-sabotage and the cycle of abuse lasted well into my 30s. I became a master of disassociation to survive.

Sexual Abuse

In the previous chapter, you read about the events leading up to me going to live with my grandparents in Erie, Pennsylvania. A few weeks in, my grandmother set me up on a date with a 30-year-old man who I was told coached baseball at a local college. I was under the impression that this was an attempt to connect with adults who could offer guidance and mentorship. As it turns out, that was not what this guy had in mind.

He picked me up, exchanged a few words with my grandmother, and we left to grab a bite to eat. After dinner, he drove me to a motel where he said he was living while his home was being remodeled. I became uncomfortable and asked him to take me home, but he told me my grandparents knew where we were and were coming to pick me up. He convinced me to go to his room to use his phone to call them (there were no cell phones back then).

I did not have time to reach the phone before he threw me on the bed and pinned my arms down. Terrified and paralyzed with fear, I was unable to speak. Feeling helpless, I kept turning my head as he tried to kiss me with his bushy red mustache. He proceeded to rape me repeatedly.

Finally, he stopped and told me to get in the car and he drove me home after my grandparents had gone to sleep. The next morning, they asked me how the date went, and I told them it was not a date, and that I doubted we would ever hear from him. No one asked me anything further, and I never spoke about it again until now. The roots of shame grew stronger and I got very good at stuffing my feelings down where I could not feel them.

Same Man, Different Face

There is a fairly new term used to explain the behavior of emotional abusers – love-bombing. Love-bombing is a manipulation technique that abusers use in the early stages of a relationship. They shower you with love and affection. They fill all of your emotional buckets. They express deep feelings of love and adoration for you and continue to make you feel special. There is not a single person in this world who does not like the way it feels to be loved in this way. This is the hook that traps so many empaths and injured souls.

By putting you on a pedestal and fulfilling your romantic needs, you feel so loved and consumed by them that you become blind to any changes. At that point, they do not have to change. All they do is stop love-bombing and their true, abusive self comes out, but you become too blinded to see it. Unfortunately, I fell victim to this behavior not once, but over and over again.

I married right out of university. We had a short courtship and got married before we left State College. Imagine my surprise when one year into the marriage, I learned that I was pregnant. I took this as a sign from God that I was meant to be a mother, and I was elated.

The pregnancy was hard on me. I was hospitalized for hyperemesis three times during the pregnancy. However, the physical complications of pregnancy were not the only things that changed in my life. My husband also changed. The details are not important, except to say he became self-centered and cruel. When I confronted him about it, he would tell me it was my hormones, and I was overreacting.

I hit a breaking point when my daughter was three months old and his behavior had become intolerable and I became afraid. Divorce was not something I was going to consider, so we tried counselling. I was hopeful and practiced every exercise suggested. Somewhere around 12 weeks into counselling, our therapist told us she did not think she could help us.

Stunned, we asked why? Then she asked if either of us knew what narcissism was. We gave our simple understanding and then she gave us her explanation. Reaching around to pick up a book, she suggested we read it and then told us she believed my husband had Narcissistic Personality Disorder (NPD), and the only way our marriage could survive was if he wanted to change and got individual, professional help. My husband dismissed her as a quack, blamed me for turning her against him, and refused to acknowledge it.

As I did research on NPD, the alarm bells went off as I saw him in everything I read. It quickly became clear that I could not help him, and he was becoming more abusive and I knew my daughter was in jeopardy.

The last straw was finding him bathing our daughter. I walked in and the water was up to her chin. I overreacted and scolded him, saying it would just take a distraction for her to slip under and drown. Of course, he insisted she loved it and that I was crazy. Getting divorced was not something I had seen for my future, but at this point, I believed there was no other option.

As a young, single mother, I believed I was more unlovable now than ever before. I put all my energy into my 18-month-old daughter and never dealt with the drama from a failed marriage, my choices, or the emotional abuse. Some would say it is no surprise I tripped again.

My second husband was a good friend who was always super protective of me. When he finally showed his true colors, I dismissed the mean names and personal attacks. After all, I reasoned he was from New York, and that was how they talked. I would not admit to myself that he might be abusive or that I had chosen wrong again.

One day, we were at the Los Angeles County Fair with my parents and my son, who was about two years old. My husband took the stroller and threw it down a hill with my son in it. Everyone saw, and no one could believe what had just happened. My stepfather was outraged. Thankfully, my son was not physically hurt.

Shortly after that incident, the gaslighting intensified and my husband started referring to me as motherf***ing c*** (MFC). Every time he would refer to me, he would call me MFC, and it became my name, even around my kids. To this day, he still calls me MFC, and we have been divorced for twenty years.

I hid the abuse, and on the outside, I was the perfect wife—like June Cleaver on steroids. I had a full-time job as a national sales director, sat on the board of directors for our local community center, had three children, was a Girl Scout and Cub Scout leader, cooked breakfast for crowds after Sunday school, and always hosted holidays. Secretly, my home life was insanity, but I did not want to have another failed marriage. I thought, "How could I be this messed up?"

When you are dealing with people who have NPD or are emotionally abusive, you cannot change them. They must want to change themselves, and intentionally work on changing.

My second husband did some horrible things, but to me, the worst was forcing me to have an abortion. This still hurts me today, and I still grieve for that baby. His reasoning was that if we cannot get along, we should not bring another child into the world. This should have been a red flag that he was not willing to work on our marriage, but I was prepared to keep trying. Less than a year later, I got pregnant with my third son. This time, I put my foot down and would not consider the alternative.

The verbal and emotional abuse got worse. One weekend, I was in Las Vegas for work and my husband was going to meet me there a few days later. Before he arrived, I met someone and, for the first time in six years, I felt like I might not be so terrible.

If just talking to a stranger could light me up inside, something was really wrong. When my husband got there, I told him we needed to talk, and something needed to change. I explained that I met someone who talked to me with respect and made me feel seen. He called me some choice words, grabbed his suitcase, and went home. We got divorced.

Today, I know I was suffering from C-PTSD and, with all the years of trauma in my early life, my thinking and coping skills were questionable. That explains but does not excuse my behavior nor the choices I made next.

Months after my second marriage ended, I started seeing a man who repeatedly tried to kill me. He was fun, loved playing outdoors with my kids, and had lots of energy. His genius mind intrigued me, and he always made me feel beautiful.

Over time, I let him move into my house and, not long after that, the violence began. The first time, he threw a beer can at my ear while I was lying in bed sleeping. Smack! I was awake and my eardrum was damaged. What in the world was that? The next day, remorse was strong, excuses believable, and he begged hard for my forgiveness.

I wanted to believe the beer can incident was an "accident", so I let it go.

I was so embarrassed that someone I chose would intentionally hurt me that I did not say anything to anyone. Even after the black eyes, bruised arms, and busted lips, I made excuses. The roots of shame went deeper still, and I was trapped. I remember thinking, "How can a smart and successful woman like me be caught up in a relationship that puts me in danger?" Maybe I deserved it. Maybe I really am crazy. Maybe.

This chaos continued for eighteen months. It was obvious to my exes, my family, and my friends I was being beaten. Why did no one offer to help me or suggest a way out? At one point, I called the local domestic violence shelter but learned I could lose my children if I went there. Again, I felt helpless.

Here is a critical lesson. The violence is not a mistake. One time is not one time. It is only one time until it happens again and again.

Rebounding, I met my third husband. He reminded me of who I used to be. I felt normal again for the first time in two years. He had a good job, two kids around the same age as mine, loved adventure and travelling, was generous with his time, and, most importantly, was very romantic. I loved him and believed he was going to be my ticket to moving on in a normal, non-violent relationship. I believed he was my savior.

Talk about love-bombing – this guy was a pro. We went through cycles of love-bombing and unhealthy behaviors for three years of dating. I should have been a pro by now and known to run. Instead, I was the perfect target and wanted to be loved so badly, I agreed to get married. Once we were married, the emotional abuse increased and the gaslighting started. He was controlling and emotionally abusive to me and my children and would spin stories about me to my friends and family to get them to side against me.

We were separated for four or five years before he agreed to file for divorce. He did not want to get divorced and, while separated and living in different states and countries, he would tell people we were still married because he wanted control over me. Divorce should always be a last resort. However, it is sometimes necessary when your emotional or physical well-being are in danger.

Emotional abuse hurts more than broken bones and bruises. I know. I have experienced it all. I also know that when in an abusive and toxic relationship, the victim will eventually believe they are to blame and deserve whatever they get. Your thoughts and shame keep you trapped. Your empathy and capacity to love beyond measure keep you trying.

A common theme with many victims of domestic violence and emotional abuse is thinking you did something to deserve the abuse. Remember, you are responsible for your words, actions, and responses. You are not responsible for how someone else treats you, and you do not have to and should never tolerate it.

A wise sage once told me, "We teach others how to treat us."

Coping Through Dissociation

You may have heard about dissociation. It allows victims of abuse to repress memories to survive. It is the survival response that helps your mind numb the events you have experienced and cope with them in a way that helps you get through the situation.

When you do not have the resources to help you cope with your experiences constructively, you enter this cycle where your perception of acceptance changes. You develop learned helplessness. People exposed to trauma repeatedly often fall into this cycle.

Learned helplessness is a destructive way to cope or survive. It becomes so ingrained that you become unable to see your destructive path. You may be able to look at others going through similar experiences to you and acknowledge that they need help, but you cannot see it in yourself because you have accepted that nothing can change, so why bother trying. This helplessness impacts your ability to choose healthy relationships or make healthy decisions.

The way you process pain and feelings determines how you learn to thrive. As a victim, I blocked out vulnerability. To me, that was weakness, and I needed to be strong. Even crying was difficult for me. I realized later that I had a hard time crying because I had numbed that part of my emotional system. I had become so good at getting hurt that I no longer recognized danger nor felt the pain.

A big part of healing and transformation is learning how to embrace being vulnerable and being brave enough to own your part in it all. Whole-minded living and healthy problem-solving come from being brave and genuinely accepting yourself. When you can take your stories and own them, you can change them.

When I had my transformational breakthrough, I experienced an emotional and physical change. I felt grief from the death of who I was pretending to be and the new life of who I really was. It was if I shed my skin and became a new person.

If you have been abused, I have good news for you. There is hope. You can heal from the pain of your past and learn how to live in an emotionally strong way. The process is not easy and there will be many layers to deal with, but I promise you it is worth it.

If you would like to find out more about how I dealt with the abuse of my past, I encourage you to take one of my masterclasses, which show you how to confront your past and move forward with your life. Go to www.sharilueck.com and check it out.

Shari Lueck

Chapter 6:

Addiction

"Character cannot be developed in ease and quiet. Only through experience of trial and suffering can the soul be strengthened, ambition inspired, and success achieved."

Helen Keller

I remember the first time I tried a mood-altering drug. I was 12 and my aunt gave me a joint to smoke before a movie. Out of curiosity, my best friends and I smoked it. I remember thinking to myself, "How can anyone like this stuff? It's horrible." Yet many years later, I was using recreational drugs and alcohol almost daily to help me get through life.

Some people turn to drinking as a crutch they think will help them get through hard days. If they encounter someone that causes them stress, or have a rough time with something, an alcoholic might think, "I'm going to drink about that" or "I need to get drunk after dealing with this."

My experience with addiction, drinking, and drugs is quite different than what is common in recovery. I have never had the feeling I need to get drunk after a stressful event or encounter. Do not get me wrong; I have had plenty to drink, but I have never had a barometer. I am one of those people who tends to think, "If a little is good, then a lot must be better."

When I was teenager, I would drink in social settings and, without warning nor any indicators, I would end up blackout drunk. By blackout, I mean I would be fully functioning on the outside and seem "fine" to the casual observer, but I would have zero recollection of the events that occurred once I had crossed that line. How stupid, dangerous, and terrifying it was. Not that this is an excuse, but I think it has a lot to do with my exposure. I was a teenager in Los Angeles, so drinking and partying on the weekends was normal. However, for me, drinking and doing drugs were more to fit in and be social rather than coping emotionally. Up to the worst part of my addiction, never did I do those substances alone.

In recovery, this is not unique, but to someone with no experience with alcoholism or addiction, I never thought of my behaviour as a "problem." Even after I got clean and sober, I did not identify as an alcoholic. The AA Big Book has an excerpt that addresses this kind of thinking: *"Despite all we can say, many who are real alcoholics are not going to believe they are in that class. By every form of self-deception and experimentation, they will try to prove themselves exceptions to the rule, therefore nonalcoholic. If anyone who is showing inability to control his drinking can do the right- about-face and drink like a gentleman, our hats are off to him. Heaven knows, we have tried hard enough and long enough to drink like other people!"*

In the throes of my addiction at age 36, I was drinking almost every day. When I was snorting white powder up my nose, the alcohol would counteract it. However, I did not think at the time I had a problem with alcohol, even though I have identified as an alcoholic several times in my life. I have always been able to put down a drink and walk away from it without an issue, and a bottle of alcohol could go unfinished in my home for years. My problem with alcohol is that when I drink, I do not always know when to stop.

The problem is that there are many people like me who think drinking excessively is acceptable and they do not have a problem because "It's just social." Whether it is social or not, it is still a problem.

Identifying as an addict was easier for me because I was absolutely chemically and physically addicted to meth. Years later, when I found AA, I discovered a whole new prescription for living that I wish had happened earlier. It is a great philosophy of living that I wish everyone would follow. If I had been exposed to AA earlier in life, my fall to rock bottom might have looked a little different on the climb back up.

Addiction Is Accidental

My first drink was a whiskey sour. I remember it like it happened this morning. I was thirteen, and every weekend there was a Bar or Bat Mitzvah party. The day I had that first drink, I remember falling up the stairs when I got home from the party. My parents laughed at me and I went to bed because I was a mess.

It was years later in high school when I tried alcohol again. I never felt like I fit in anywhere, so drinking helped me feel less self-conscious and was a way of hanging out with my friends. We smoked pot occasionally and drank a lot, but I never touched any harder drugs.

I wonder why I was so convicted about not doing "hard" drugs when I was young. After all, this was Los Angeles in the 80s, where famous people threw big parties and cocaine was readily available. My friends would do cocaine, but I did not, and they would sometimes tease me about it. However, I knew someone who had died the first time he tried cocaine, and that stuck in my head for a long time. For him, it was a "one and done" deal. As I grew up, my coping techniques were focused on other types of addictions and obsessions, like shopping.

Many people have asked me how I survived life in Los Angeles in the 80s without touching cocaine because it seemed that wherever we were, it was always there. People would carry it around in little brown vials with tiny gold spoons so they could do it in bathrooms or at parties. I have been to wild parties, and through the Playboy Mansion, and still never touched it. I used to find myself questioning why I decided almost twenty years later it would be a good idea.

I guess, up to that point, my other skeletons and coping mechanisms worked out fine. However, as life spiraled down and I ended up in the worst abuse situation ever, it went beyond what I could deal with given the skills I had.

Shortly after my children had experienced the shooting, I lost my job as an executive, my husband divorced me, and everything spiraled out of control. I was at a small dinner party and someone took out some cocaine. I remember thinking, "Life sucks anyway. What difference does it make?" I did a line and then did some more. It was amazing and I suddenly felt like I was normal. What a lie!

At the time, I was in a soon-to-become abusive relationship. I was with him and his friends when I did that first line of cocaine. This should have been a sign I was with someone who did not care about me and who should not be anywhere near me or my children, but I was sick. Many people still do not understand mental illness, and it is not obvious when someone is suffering internally. My PTSD was full blown, and I was clinically depressed and riddled with anxiety.

When I snorted cocaine for the first time, everything felt normal again and that is all I wanted. I knew I should not touch it anymore because, in my way of thinking, a little is never enough. However, a few weeks later, I did it again. This time I knew I had to stop because I realized how much I liked it.

Weekends turned into weekdays and cocaine quickly became a crutch. I felt better, was thinking clearly, and was more creative. Coke turned into meth and I was hooked.

Later, I learned I have Attention Deficit Disorder (ADD), which explains why I reacted this way. This is why many people with ADD and ADHD end up becoming drug addicts. They are put on Ritalin as kids and teens, which has the same addictive effect, and once they turn eighteen, they are taken off Ritalin cold turkey. There is no proper withdrawal period. Then their brains continue to crave that feeling, and they turn to drugs. Studies have shown that about 95% of kids who are on Ritalin end up becoming drug addicts.

Once cocaine became a physical addiction for me, I was overcome with shame. I felt too ashamed to be in this world, and I did not want anyone to know and I did not know where to look for help. At the time, I had only known about Narcotics Anonymous (NA) but believed this was primarily for on-the-street heroin addicts.

Then, I heard about AA, but thought it was only for alcoholics. When I found out I could go to AA, I was worried someone might recognize me there. In my shame, I did not consider that if someone were there and recognized me, they would also be there for their own addiction. All I could think about was my own shame.

As much as I tried to hide it, everyone knew what I was going through. No one reached out to help me. I was caught in this loop of shame, not knowing how to get help because I did not believe that I fit into a specific category.

Addiction Is Life in Chaos

There is a stigma around people who have addictions, but it is absurd. No one becomes an addict on purpose. Nobody starts using drugs because they think, "Geez, you know what, I would like to be a drug addict. Yes, that sounds like a great idea." They use drugs or alcohol to meet a need or cover up a feeling or loss in their life and before they know it, without warning, they are addicted.

Life in the deepest part of my addiction was pure chaos. My personality changed. I suffered from lack of sleep, and nights became days. All I could think about was seeking out the next thrill. I still had responsibilities, but I went from being a hyper-focused, diligent person to not caring about a lot of things. I let a lot of stuff roll off my back that I should not have let go.

It was easy for me to become angry, and sometimes I would go into a rage and break things. I started hanging out with people I would never have associated with before, and I put up with things I should not have. My boyfriend severely abused me, and the drugs became a way to numb the abuse.

Instead of caring about life, I only cared about feeling good. I became a walking, talking tornado and creator of chaos. The drugs tricked me into thinking that I was finally happy and enjoying life. Even though it was dangerous to me and everyone around me, I did not think about that. I did not feel endangered until I started feeling suicidal.

There were many times I felt that I wanted to die. The shame and pain that came with my addiction would often become overwhelming and I did not think I belonged on earth. I believed the lies my ex would tell my kids that I was a useless and disgusting piece of trash.

A common misconception about suicide is that many people believe it is selfish, or taking the easy way out, but someone who is suicidal does not see it that way. The deception of suicide is believing you are doing others a favour by taking yourself out of the equation. In a suicidal person's mind, they are not being selfish at all. They believe they are sacrificing themselves so that everyone around them can have a better life.

Everything stems from experiencing a kind of pain that does not make sense. You can look back at your own life and think, "Well, maybe if I had done this thing differently, I would not have ended up this way." However, it comes down to mental wellness.

To get out of addiction, you have to be able to change your way of thinking. The mindset that got you into drugs in the first place is not the mindset that will help you get out of them. I had no reason to change my thinking, so instead I began to think if I removed myself from the situation, my family and children would be better off. In my mind, I was the problem.

Putting Your Inner Tornado to Rest

In the previous chapter, I mentioned that after finally leaving my abusive ex-boyfriend and getting a fresh start in a new home, he climbed up the balcony and broke into my home to attack me. Before this incident, I was truly trying to make changes and get out of my situation. I knew if I stayed how I was, I would either end up in jail, killing myself or being killed. Regardless of the reason, I needed to get back to my old life if I was going to survive.

After my ex-boyfriend broke into my home and attacked me, I knew that could not happen again. I had to take my life back. Drugs could no longer be a solution. I could see how drugs destroyed my life and recognized I would not be able to raise my children in a healthy, positive environment if I continued down this path.

I saw an Oprah episode with James Frey, author of *A Million Little Pieces*. He was discussing his book and how he had singlehandedly gotten clean and sober and freed himself from his meth addiction. I immediately bought the book. When I read *A Million Little Pieces*, I recognized this man had what I considered at the time to be a bigger problem with addiction than I did. I thought that if he could get off meth on his own, then so could I, and I decided to stop.

I arranged to have my kids stay with their father, and I spent a week with an intense sickness coming off the drugs. It felt like the worst flu I had ever had. I felt like I was going to die, and I wanted to kill myself, but my kids kept me going.

I suffered from withdrawal for almost a week. I was sick and scared, but I muscled through. Life did not immediately get better once I stopped doing drugs. I was doing this on my own and had no one to talk to about it. Quitting drugs meant I had to give up everything I had associated with drugs, like certain people or places I used to go. Those people and places had become my whole life, and I fell into a different kind of isolation and depression.

My kids were my miracle babies who had already gone through so much pain. They lived through the abuse and addiction and saw their mom change in front of their eyes. It was never fair to them, and this was an integral part of my recovery and my motivation for getting my life together.

You do not get do-overs in life. When an addict is in the throes of addiction, they are unable to see the impact of their addiction on the people around them. A functioning addict believes that their actions do not impact anyone because they are still able to function normally in their minds.

When I was a functioning addict, I had enough financial stability to keep my nanny. I still sent my kids to school, fed them, and had them do their homework, but I was out all night. Since I was still able to provide my kids with a "normal" life, I did not think I was affecting them. However, when I got clean, I realized I had been impacting them significantly.

One night, I did not come home at all. My daughter woke up and was scared because her nanny was there, but her mom was not. She will still say to this day that she felt abandoned. For me, this is a big deal because I went through substantial abandonment issues that started in childhood.

It was not until years later that I could see what I had done to my kids when they were younger. We did not talk about this at the time, but we talk about it now. Many addicts do not take the time to listen to the people in their lives who can see them slowly killing themselves.

You Can Set Yourself Free

The cycles of abuse and the cycles of addiction are similar. I have lived through both.

Gaslighting usually happens in an abusive relationship. The abuser is charming to everyone else, so you as the victim begin to believe you are the crazy one. Then you become stuck in a circle; you get stuck in your own story and take the poison from your abuser. It comes in daily doses, so it does not kill you right away or knock you out. Instead, it kills you slowly and a little more each day, until one day you get the right dose, and it takes you out.

You will not know which dose is going to be the final one until it is too late.

When you do not change the things in your life that create chaos, you accept a slow dose of poison and slowly kill yourself. Staying in a bad situation means you are actively choosing to take the poison and continue this path. It will kill your soul.

A few years ago, I decided I wanted to lose weight. Around Thanksgiving, a friend told me to go to the grocery store and pick up frozen turkeys to see what the different weights felt like. I went to the store, picked up a 13-pound turkey, and walked around with it for a while. When I tried this with a 22-pound turkey, I could not make it as far. Putting down the 22-pound turkey showed me how heavy it truly was.

Finding freedom felt like dropping the weight of that turkey I was carrying around. When I found freedom, I felt lighter and I could see hope where I could not before. That hope had never gone away, but now I was able to see and feel things I had not felt in a long time. Emotions became more extreme, so I had to learn how to cope with them instead of hiding them away.

So many people squash their emotions and avoid showing the feelings that are described as inappropriate, such as anger or sadness. However, these emotions are necessary. When you learn how to feel them effectively, you can work through them and find your own freedom.

To me, freedom is the quest to have a sense of peace and calm in yourself. I have it, and you can, too. Everyone deserves to have it.

Emotions are a way of working through recovery as well. We are all a reflection of one another, so if you recognize an emotion in someone else, it is because you have that emotion in ourselves. In recovery, there is a saying: "If you spot it, you've got it." If you spot judgmental behaviour in someone else, for example, it is because you recognize judgment in yourself.

I understand now how to feel the emotions that I am feeling, and how they can serve me. Now, I can adjust the story I am telling to remind myself that I feel calm and peaceful.

Sometimes you will have negative voices in your head, and you need to learn how to recognize and quiet those voices. Through emotional healing, you learn how to eliminate the physical and emotional needs behind it.

If you are struggling with alcohol or addiction, I promise that getting clean is worth it. The shame you carry, and hide does go away. Inside the rooms of AA, there is love and understanding. There are people from all walks of life, and they will love you until you can love yourself.

Thanks to the Internet, there are many resources to guide you toward help. Please use them. Nobody should live in fear or suffer alone. Your life matters and you have a purpose to fulfill.

Your mind plays tricks on you. Your self-talk and self-doubt reinforce the negative beliefs you believe about yourself. Today, one thing I find helpful when I feel anxious or out of sorts is to listen to guided meditation or guided affirmations. It is a solid option for instant calm and allowing your mind to wander.

Shari Lueck

Chapter 7:

Grief

*Life seems sometimes like nothing more than a series
of losses, from beginning to end. That's the given.
How you respond to those losses, what you make of
what's left, that's the part you have to make up as
you go.*
Katharine Weber

I almost always associated grief with death in the past, never with loss. Then something changed and I shifted.

When I was 47, I learned what grief is. I was sitting in a coaching group doing a grief exercise, and everyone around me was crying as the leader talked and prompted us to visualize our grief. Nothing was coming up for me. I was not tapping into anything that felt like grief. I guess, at the time, I believed I had already accepted my grief or that I did not have any, so I felt fine.

After the exercise, however, I was challenged by my peers to think about it, reframe it, and what followed next was a reflection on a lifetime filled with dismissed grief.

I often wonder what my life would have been like if I had allowed myself to feel grief and deal with it at the time, or if I had let it heal later instead of burying it deep inside me. I had been told so many times as a child and young adult, "Just get over it and accept it," or "What's done is done." It became a core part of who I was and how I processed or, in this case, ignored important emotions.

Grief is not organic or linear, and it does not have rules or a timeline. Everyone deals with grief differently, and you can only heal by letting yourself feel it, sit with it, and experience it.

The Dark Path After Grief and Loss

Most people are familiar with the five stages of grief: denial, anger, bargaining, depression, and acceptance. In 2019, David Kessler came out with a sixth stage of grief, which is finding meaning after a loss. Before this point, talking about grief as a form of loss was not generally accepted, but now it is starting to gain momentum.

All trauma loss can be associated with grief. Therefore, all trauma often creates a grief emotion.

Grief and loss can lead you to low points. Some people like to call this rock bottom, but for me, my rock was always rubber. I bounced between many different low points in my life.

I believe the lowest point in my life was the two years that followed the shooting at the Jewish Community Center. The outpouring of grief I experienced after that incident was immense. I went through that first stage of denial, thinking, "What just happened? This cannot be real. There was a shooting at the Jewish Community Center. Let's find out if it was our Jewish Community Center. Oh, my God, it is our Jewish Community Center, and the kids are there." As those thoughts went racing through my mind, I was paralyzed.

When I got to the scene, I was the first civilian there. The rest of the people on site were first responders, some of whom tackled me to the ground when I cut through the yellow tape. I recognize today that my own grief experience was likely different from the others standing beside me that day.

Following the incident, when we met with grief counsellors, they focused on the fact that no one died. It felt unfair. To me, life as I knew it changed completely in that moment. This is grief. I was grieving the loss of my previous life and the fact that nothing would be the same anymore. It took me more than a decade to process the grief I carried after that day.

There is a difference between the way we deal with grief individually and collectively. After this mass shooting, everyone involved dealt with a collective grief, and we did some group healing exercises together. At the same time, grief affected everyone differently.

My grief manifested irrationally, and in ways that still hurt me to this day. I felt I was to blame because I had chosen to send my kids to that community center. It was like I had taken a massive boulder to the head, and I later learned it was likely a compound effect of all the pain from the loss I had experienced throughout my life without properly dealing with my grief.

Following the shooting, I had a lot of loss in a one-year span. I got divorced, I lost my job, I lost my house, and then 9/11 happened, which triggered more fear in me. My kids were also dealing with this loss, and as their mother, I was affected exponentially. They had to do their own healing, and throughout my journey of healing, they have learned to cope in their way. Yet, there is more work to be done.

How Do You Deal With Your Grief?

Since you all grieve differently, you tend to judge others on how they grieve. You might think people are moving on too quickly or not quickly enough, or they are overreacting. This can be isolating for the person who is grieving.

That judgment of grieving is what I believe led to my second divorce. When two people are grieving, you cannot be each other's grief counsellor because there will end up being judgment on both sides, and judgment kills relationships.

Judgment demands punishment, either internally or externally. When your partner judges you externally, shame sets in and begins to take root. Once shame takes root, it becomes difficult to pull it out. If you do not recognize it soon enough, it grows and becomes suffocating. Grief is a mirror of love. Everything heals with love. You cannot get rid of shame if you do not replace it with love.

Often, you do not know what you had until it is gone, so you will not always recognize the loss right away. This can apply to anything, not only relationships. It could happen if you lose a job. After all, losing a job is a lot like losing your identity, and in the aftermath, it is common to feel as though you will never be the same even when you find your identity again.

I remember the first time I got fired. It shattered me at my core. The termination was total BS and fabricated lies. The owner of the company knew it. So, they offered me a severance I could not refuse. They offered to pay me $10,000 per month for twelve months. I believed it was obvious the termination had nothing to do with me since they were still paying me. However, the people around me acted as though I had done something wrong instead of feeling sympathy or empathy for me. My ex-husband told my children I was a total loser because I got fired from my job. How embarrassing.

At the time, I was still healing from the grief I had experienced after the shooting. Everyone I worked with who had been like family to me suddenly turned their backs on me after I lost my job. All the grief and judgment that came from the outside became unbearable. I could not talk about it because I had signed an agreement with my former employer, so I started carrying that blame and shame.

After losing my job, I lost my friends, family, home, and livelihood and I felt like my kids' housing security was put at risk. That was a lot of loss and a lot of grief. I can still feel the weight of the memory today as I write.

The Grief Cycle Is Not One-Size-Fits-All

The grief cycle is not linear, and it is not the same for everyone. It is a scaffolding you climb across and rebuild. Everyone experiences grief differently, and everyone is affected by it in their own way.

Anger is one of the stages of grief. It is not always part of the grieving process, but it is an important emotion.

I kept so much grief bottled up over the years. I think it escaped as anger. Sometimes I would get so angry that it looked and felt like rage, but it did not make sense. As an adult, something would set me off, and I would overreact, sometimes flying into a rage, and there were times I would be so frustrated I would break things.

Instead of feeling my anger and experiencing it, I became afraid of it. So, I would shove it down until I could not handle it anymore and I would fly off the handle. Occasionally, if provoked by my partner(s) ignoring or making excuses and dismissing me, anger would bottle up and act out. The pain was overwhelming and feeling invisible or ignored was a huge trigger. I wanted it to go away.

My addictions were also the result of my unhealed grief. I think numbing was the only way to make the pain go away. Truth be told, although the pain never left, I did not care about it anymore.

Depression can be another part of the grief cycle, and I am not talking about sadness. There is a big difference between feeling sad and being depressed, and then there is clinical depression. Clinical depression needs to be treated to help it go away. There are so many people today suffering from depression and they have days they cannot even take a shower without feeling overwhelmed. You start to cancel your appointments because you cannot bring yourself to attend them. Dishes pile up in the sink, laundry goes undone, meals do not get prepared… you get it, it's crippling.

Finding Meaning After a Loss

Grief is something we cannot hide from and should not ignore. If we do, it will come out one way or another. No matter how far down you shove the grief and try to hide or mask your feelings, it still lives inside you. Eventually, if left to its own devices, it will attack you.

When dealing with grief, I suggest looking for little wins in the moment. For example, let's say you lost your job. You feel like your livelihood has been stripped away and fear has taken over. If you are able to start the job search, or work on your resume, this would be a good win to recognize because you are addressing that loss. If you are suffering from depression, taking a shower might be a small win for the day.

Looking for those little wins can help you recognize what you are feeling and the emotions you are going through so you can get to the other side.

My younger sister died five years ago. Thankfully, I learned to deal with grief before she died, so I was able to grieve her death properly and find meaning in the love we shared. I still miss her to this day, and her death affected me in a big way. However, thanks to the healing I have done, I was able to come to terms and cherish the memories I had with her.

If you heal properly, you can experience a healthy grieving cycle and find meaning from your loss. Believe it or not, I am excited because in the next chapter I get to share my healing journey and the amazing things that have happened in it.

Shari Lueck

Chapter 8:

Finding God and Connection

"Peace does not lie in getting God to give me other circumstances. Peace lies in finding God in these circumstances."
John Ortberg

I have often heard people say that the things you go through in life happen to teach you a lesson. In my opinion, life is not about a series of lessons. Instead, it is about finding your place and using God's will to guide you in the right direction. Every decision you make can be made according to your ego or faith. The choice is yours.

Growing up, I questioned the idea of God. Yes, even after having a Bat Mitzvah, a part of me still questioned. I had a hard time understanding why God would let terrible things happen like racism, war, and murder.

I have a different understanding today. Bad things will always happen. Evil is out there in the world and it always will be as long as there are people who choose to fan its flames. God is here to guide you through the hard times and help you find the light in the darkness.

I think that most humans question their faith at some point in time. Even those who were raised with a strong, unwavering faith have questions. If you find yourself with some questions, understand that this is normal and okay. You are here with free will to choose what you believe. I have learned that accepting a higher power into your life will allow you to shape the world you wish to live in and guide you when you are lost.

The Day I Met God

While in recovery rooms and working with others, I would always hear, "Get on your knees and pray. Until you are willing to hit the floor and get on your knees, you're not going to get any change. You're not going to meet God until you get on your knees."

However, being raised in a Jewish home, I was always told not to pray on my knees and my mother reinforced that during my time in Catholic high school. Later in life, I was resistant to the idea, so I never thought I would meet God the way others had. With practice, however, I eventually embraced the idea of a Higher Power and learned to listen for guidance. It was not long before I realized I could have a conversation with God from anywhere. I could even be in a public bathroom and still talk to God.

After getting sober, I looked for more ways to strengthen my faith, and I even got down on my knees to pray. Lightning did not strike me, but it did make a difference. I started to recognize signs and could feel the energy shift in the mornings when I prayed to follow God's will and not mine. My relationship with God was good, but all of that changed when Jeff Class came into my life.

Jeff and I met by divine intervention. He called me out of the blue after seeing my resume online in 2003. I refused to meet with him, but he was persistent. Finally, after three attempts, I agreed to "talk." That day turned out to be the beginning of an amazing career and friendship.

Jeff is a devout Christian with a strong faith. As my mentor, we talked a lot about God and had some magical conversations that opened my eyes and helped me succeed in all areas of my life. I grew to rely on Jeff's wisdom and discovered a newfound view when he shared a biblical or Godly point of view. He was never preachy, but he was a terrific storyteller, as his parables always made sense.

Occasionally, we would pray together. To this day, listening to Jeff pray brings me peace. It never mattered what he was praying about; it is always uplifting and peaceful. There were many times when I was challenged by my ex-husband, my teenage kids, and other relationship conflicts detailed throughout the book and Jeff would ask God to lift us all up and say other kind words. Sometimes we would pray with others and the force of togetherness was not lost on me. These experiences brought God into my life in a way I had never experienced before.

One day at work, I was going to deliver the biggest presentation to date and wanted to pray beforehand. Jeff and I always prayed before important events, sales, or presentations and miracles seemed to unfold.

Many people will scoff that we prayed at work or claim it was illegal. However, if I am not forcing nor subjecting anyone to pray, it is within my legal rights and nobody would have been the wiser. Anyway, it worked for us, but this time it was different. Prior to delivering this particular presentation to VUSD, a few of my teammates who are believers asked if they could join us. We gathered in the conference room, locked the door so we would not infringe on anyone else's beliefs, and stood and held hands.

I had heard spiritual people talk about seeing colors and sharing that the spirit chose those colors. As we began to pray, I started to feel warmth fill my body and I felt lighter than normal. It was almost as if I was weightless. Then, standing there, I dropped hands with those beside me and something magnificent happened. As my body got warmer and lighter, I saw colors. It was all I saw, like a gradient sunset of deep purples and muted magentas. Then, suddenly, I saw a bright light, and even though my body felt warm and full of love, I felt chills throughout my body, and I opened my eyes.

I stood there. According to the others in the room, I looked different. Afraid that I would get laughed at, I almost did not share my experience. Then, I decided to tell everyone I met God. I know I did, and I have not let go since that day. From that moment forward, I knew deep in my soul that everything was going to be okay.

We were all blessed in many ways, and I made the sale. At that time, it was the biggest sale I had ever made, worth $3.8 million. Jeff was a godsend to me in so many ways, and I will be forever grateful for his introduction to a loving God.

There Is Something Bigger Than Us

Whenever I start to question things, I think about Romans 8:28: "All things work together for good to those who love God, to those who are the called according to His purpose." While I have never been into Bible studies, this verse continues to comfort me and keep me going, even through difficult times.

Faith is different for everyone. Some people believe in spirit, while others believe in the higher power of the universe. I once met a man who prayed to a mango tree and called it his higher power. He told me he is a Christian but prayed to the mango tree when he was getting sober and it worked for him.

We discussed God while growing up as a child and in my home with my children, usually in terms of hate and war over the years. I remember my mother questioning why God would have let Hitler rise to power, and the Holocaust exterminate six million Jews. More recently, I have been exposed to faith that says that the end of World War II is proof that there is a God because it would not have been stopped without God.

As a family that survived a hate crime for being Jewish, my kids have gone through periods of doubt and denial. After the shooting, they did not want to be Jewish anymore. Like the Holocaust, this hate crime was the result of pure, unrestricted evil. There was no lesson to be learned. Evil can only exist if there are people to give it fuel.

There is a lot of hatred and divide today, more than I have experienced in my lifetime. The division and blame, racism, and gender bias are almost unconscionable to me. It is by pure faith that I believe things will get better, but God does not work miracles when people do not move their feet.

This is why people say, "This is little old me, but God has moved mountains, and, therefore, by the grace of God go I." While free will is where sin and evil start, it is that same free will that can stop it.

When we give ourselves to a higher power, we shut out judgment and fear, and God will talk to us. God also gives us the free will to choose what we do with our lives. One of the biggest principles they teach in recovery is that you have God's will, and you have your own will. Which one are you going to choose?

When I got sober, I would start my days with this prayer: "God, please help me live in your will today. Please guide me to get out of my own way and when I'm in doubt or I have questions, let me feel your hand on my lower back guiding me toward where I need to go." I still start my days with that prayer, and if I forget it is not long before I am reminded. At first, I questioned why someone suggested to start my day with that prayer. The answer made sense: to get out of my own way, I needed help.

Some religions present God as a punishing God, which causes some people to fear God. Others talk about a loving and forgiving God. It does not matter if you believe in God or not. I know for me life became easier when I surrendered to something bigger than me. God does not have to be one thing or another, and He is not scary. When you accept that there is a higher power, and you follow and honor that higher power, you become a better person and have the ability to make a positive difference.

So, whether your higher power is God, the universe, a spirit or a mango tree, everything will make sense when you surrender to the idea that there is something bigger than yourself. This does not mean there is no sin nor evil in the world. All you have to do is turn on the news or take a look at social media to see that.

It is not my place, nor anyone else's place, to tell you how to pray or what to believe. Only you know how a higher power plays a role in your life. Today, God is an important and powerful force in my life, and He has given me strength when nothing else could.

Choose Your Happiness Over Your History

Your past does not have to be your future. I know this with certainty. It does not come on its own; you have to do the work. You have to be willing to feel through the pain and range of emotions you have stuffed down or numbed to survive.

Life with unhealed trauma or addiction is pure chaos. It is an emotional roller coaster of highs and lows and a lot of noise, mostly self-made. One thing that gets shut down is the ability to trust yourself. I mentioned in a previous chapter that my governor was broken, and I always discounted my intuition or second guessed my decisions.

You know about negative self-talk. It's that nagging voice in your head that tells you that you are not good enough. You will never amount to anything. What you want does not matter. Nobody cares. You are not lovable. You have to stay small to stay safe, and the list goes on and on. This challenges us and fills us with constant self-doubt, which is often paired with self-loathing.

That inner voice can be mean. You would not talk to a friend like this, so why would you talk to yourself this way? This is what keeps you in that circle of fear. You become so comfortable in the status quo that you do not challenge it because you are afraid of losing what you have. The self-talk and fear created an inability to set healthy boundaries because I relied on the opinion of others to validate that I was worthy.

My relationships were not based on admiration and trust. Instead, they were dictated by fear. I was afraid that people did not like me, let alone love me. Walking around as an imposter in my own life, I worried that if I let someone in, they would see the real me, and see that there was something wrong with me. Fearful that I would be left alone and scared, I believed I had to keep everyone around me happy at my own expense. It was not only exhausting, but it caused devastation for me and those around me.

The loneliness, the horrible relationships, and the self-doubt all followed me. They showed up at home, at work, and at play. It did not matter what I changed; those things haunted me supported by my negative self-talk. What I wanted more than anything was connection, and I was the reason I did not have it. Thank God, I broke the cycle. I learned to set and hold boundaries for the first time and discovered the joy in being able to ask for what I needed and allowed myself to receive it. I learned how to give and receive love.

When I look back at the course of my life, I can see there were times I severed ties and broke connections in an attempt to actually make connections. The key to changing this cycle is setting boundaries for yourself. Recognize what works for you and what brings you joy, and then honor your commitment to yourself.

Boundaries teach other people how to treat you. For example, if you are in a romantic relationship and you let your partner raise their voice and yell at you, they will learn subconsciously you do not have a problem with it. This gives them the green light to continue treating you badly. Instead of questioning why people were treating me badly, I used to question myself. I believed something was wrong with me and I deserved to be treated badly because I would listen to my self-talk.

Often, when people get angry and raise their voice, they use the defense they are being passionate. I am a deeply passionate person, and I can talk loud and fast when I am excited about something. However, passion does not insult or hurt another person. If someone tells me that my tone of voice is making them uncomfortable, I will not excuse it and continue to berate them. I want that connection, so I will put the brakes on and change my behavior.

Now when something or someone does not feel quite right, I get still and peaceful, and tune in to my self-worth. One of my favorite sayings is from Psalm 46:10: "Be still and know that I am God." It is written on my coffee cup and on my computer screen and reminds me to always be patient and still. There were many years I left a category five hurricane of destruction along my path. Had I taken a time out, been still, and listened to my gut, things would have been different.

As human beings, we are wired for connection. To be connected with other people truly makes life doable and fun. Whether it is a connection to a higher power or with other people, you need those connections and, ultimately, I think that they are all interwoven.

The thing about connection is you do not need to have it with everyone. I used to be so desperate to be seen and included that I wanted a connection from anyone who would give it, so I constantly put up with bad behavior. Now, if someone treats me badly, I do not want or need a connection with them because I have created healthy boundaries. Boundaries help you make the right connections and repel mistreatment.

Setting those boundaries is a core part of self-care, which forms the basis for how you receive and give love. Normally, when people describe self-care, they talk about giving yourself a spa day or getting a facial. To me, this is not self-care. This is spoiling yourself. True self-care is investing in yourself and making the decision to prioritize you, whether with your health or happiness. My version of self-care is investing in myself, making me a priority, and putting my happiness before my history.

How Will You Change Your Life?

No more shame! When you change, the world around you changes and that can easily drag you right back to where you started.

I have worked with hundreds of people who could not explain what was wrong in their life, but they were not at rock bottom. There was this overarching feeling that something was not quite right, something was missing, and that feeling seemed to exist in all areas of life. That same feeling led me to my personal breakthrough and transformation.

I experimented for years and tried changing things and implemented different solutions. I tried changing my eating habits, thinking if I ate differently or exercised more, my mental health would improve. I changed jobs, believing that the toxic environment and crazy commute was contributing to my impatience and short fuse. I tried therapy again and, as before, it left me feeling worse every week. I read every self-help book I could get my hands on and I even tried painting again. Then I moved 2,000 miles away, thinking that would fill the holes in my soul and I would rediscover who I was.

What I finally learned was that I had abandoned myself, time and time again, and I had no idea how to get her back. I can tell you this: positive thinking had nothing to do with it. There was no amount of mindset shift or positive thinking that would have made my life, my job, or my relationships better or less stressful. Positive thinking could not give me purpose again. Why? Because negative thoughts alert you that something is wrong, and that something needs to change.

Positive thinking could not solve the unresolved trauma that had left me trapped in the prison of my mind. It could not help ending my third marriage, nor remove the unhealthy people from my life. Instead, it acted like acceptance and prevented me from acknowledging my real feelings and turning inward to deal with them head on. Fear held me back and fear is never a reason to settle.

So, where do you start? It starts with you. You need to discover who you are underneath the cloak of shame you have sewn so fashionably around your shoulders. You need to find the person you were created to be, and not what society, your friends, your family, or social media is telling you to be. By the time you reach adulthood, you have already listened to your teachers, your parents, and the world, and have deviated from your authentic self to become who you think you are supposed to be.

Maybe at this point you are saying to yourself, "That is all fine and good for you, Shari. I do not have shame. I have not had any of the experiences in life you have had. What do I need to be ashamed of? I have done everything perfectly and feel like something is missing."

I promise you may not see your cloak of shame, but it is there. You add to it one fiber at a time, until you do not realize it is weighing down on you because it has slowly become part of the fabric of who you think you are.

When you walk around carrying your cloak of shame, you do not believe that anyone can see you underneath. Not being able to see it does not mean it is not there. Your shame affects everything you do and is always with you.

If you are ready to stop hiding, then you are ready to challenge the voices in your head telling you that you are not good enough, and you can start to make choices to shape and create the life you desire and deserve. You are never too old or young to start, and once you do you will be able to embrace joy, patience, peace, and connection.

A good place to begin is to treat yourself the way you want to be treated by others. If you are ready to begin the process of being set free, then Chapter 9 is for you.

Chapter 9:

Forgiveness

*"The weak can never forgive. Forgiveness is the
attribute of the strong."*
Mahatma Gandhi

W e all have courage inside of us and we use that courage to explore the world around us and make choices.

Courage is also what allows us to forgive. We do not need to forget something happened to us to move on with our lives, but we do need to learn to accept, trust, and have faith in ourselves. This all starts with forgiveness.

Forgiveness has played a significant role in my recovery and healing process, and without true forgiveness, you cannot move on towards a happy and healthy life. However, forgiveness has not always come easy and is something you need to learn before you can let go of the skeletons in your past. If I have learned to do this, so can you.

The True Power of Forgiveness

The true key to happiness is forgiveness. It is important to keep in mind, however, that forgiveness does not mean acceptance of bad behavior. People often mix the two, which is why it can be difficult for many of us to forgive others.

For example, when you marry someone, each spouse vows to remain committed and loyal to one another. If your spouse cheats on you and begins any type of romantic relationship with someone else, they betray your trust. If you choose to forgive your spouse, it does not mean that you are okay with nor accepting their bad behavior. It is still possible forgive someone even if what they did was wrong.

I think that this is where so many people get stuck in the concept and act of forgiveness. For many years, I had a hard time understanding forgiveness was an action. Instead, I thought of it as a belief. There were many times I said: "I forgive you." Deep down, I was not really forgiving them, but just trying to move past and get over whatever the behavior or act was.

132

In order to really heal our emotional wounds, forgiveness is necessary. But, in order to practice forgiveness, there are a few important things that we need to do. First, you need to learn what forgiveness really means. Psychologists generally **define forgiveness** as a conscious, deliberate decision to release feelings of resentment or vengeance toward a person or group who has harmed you, regardless of whether they actually deserve your **forgiveness.**

Just as important as defining what forgiveness *is*, though, is understanding what forgiveness is *not*. Experts who study or teach forgiveness make clear that when you forgive, you do not gloss over or deny the seriousness of an offense against you. Forgiveness does not mean forgetting, nor does it mean condoning or excusing offenses. Though forgiveness can help repair a damaged relationship, it doesn't obligate you to reconcile with the person who harmed you.

Instead, forgiveness brings the forgiver peace of mind and frees him or her from corrosive anger. It empowers you to recognize the pain you suffered without letting that pain define you, enabling you to heal and move on with your life. (Greater Good Magazine)

The hardest person to forgive is always forgiving yourself. Few definitions of self–forgiveness can be found in the social sciences literature, but those that do exist emphasize self–love and respect in the face of one's own wrongdoing. It is a lot easier to blame the things that have happened to us on other people instead taking responsibility and admitting, "I created this." (Engel)

When I was learning to forgive myself, I had a hard time with this concept. I struggled with the abuse I received and childhood pain that was the result of perceived wrongdoing. How in the world was I responsible for that bs? Seriously, this was a hard subject for me to grasp.

Ultimately, I learned to accept the fact that my parents did the best they could do and never intended to hurt me. As a parent, that was easier to understand than taking responsibility for the domestic violence I fell victim too. For that one, I needed a different lens.

Nobody deserves to be abused, not physically and not emotionally. So how was I supposed to forgive the men that abused me? What did I do to deserve getting my jaw broken? Nothing! In order to really heal, I had to take a step back and realize that I chose the man and made the decision to be in that relationship.

Even though there were no signs of abuse at the beginning of the relationship, I made excuses from the beginning for poor behavior. I did not love myself, so I settled and allowed my "partner" to fill that void for me. Then, I ultimately made the choice to stay with the man long after he became abusive. It is a lot to admit, but I had to come to terms with the fact that I was responsible for making my choices and therefore deserved forgiveness because at that time, I really did do the best I could.

Ultimately, we all should take responsibility for our choices, decisions, and our actions. When we do, it can radically change how we act in life. Had I understood what it really means to take full responsibility and review, forgive, and grow, I would have learned to forgive myself earlier in life. I would have learned how to release the shame and made better decisions and different choices.

To truly forgive yourself, you need to be willing to admit, review, and change. Once you let go of your shame, emotional relief replaces it. In previous chapters, I referred to the cloak of shame. When we hide under the cloak of shame, we convince ourselves that others who have wronged us are at fault instead of finding the courage to look ourselves in the mirror and truly forgive.

Forgiveness is a Choice

People often ask me, "How can you forgive someone that did such terrible things to you?" My answer is always,

"I truly believe they did the best they could at that time." Even if it does not seem that way, I have to believe that because I do not know what happened in someone else's life to cause them to behave in a certain way.

At 17, mother made the choice to move without me. I felt abandoned and unloved, so how did I forgive her for that? It was easier than you might think. Forgiving someone for childhood trauma, abuse, or emotional pain that happened in the past does not mean that you accept the bad behavior. Nor are you acknowledging that you deserved that harsh treatment. Instead, you are recognizing that they did the best they could at the time and forgiving them by releasing the blame you have carried around for years.

It takes courage to walk through fear and undress shame, but forgiveness is a choice. True, real forgiveness leads to healing. When you truly forgive someone, and you mean it, they cannot hurt you anymore. Sometimes people say, "Let go and let God." That is their expression encouraging the act of forgiveness.

If you do not forgive someone, you allow them to continue to hurt you and it continues to be a piece of your shame that causes you pain. Whether you realize it or not, you carry that shame with you, and it creates patterns in other areas of your life.

There are some things that I struggle to forgive. I still get angry at the shooter that came in and shot at the Jewish Community Center while my kids were there. However, for so long, I tortured myself with guilt and blame, thinking it was my fault, because I had chosen to send my kids there. Since then, I learned to forgive myself and stop letting my anger control me. In this situation, I was the person I needed to forgive.

For me, true forgiveness means leaving this shame in the dust. When you have truly forgiven something, you can talk about it without your emotions taking control. Healing helps you become neutral about a topic. People tell me all the time that things trigger them, and there are certain words that used to trigger me, too. After the shooting, the sound of a helicopter was a big trigger for me. If I heard one in the distance, I would start to let my fear take over and become tense.

If something triggers you, you have unresolved issues and have not healed from it properly. Now that I have done so much healing in my own life, I rarely become triggered by people, words, or places.

How I Learned to Forgive

A few years after I had gotten sober, I read a book called *Everything Happens for a Reason*. At the time, I was trying to understand the why and searching to find the reason in everything I had ever experienced. I think that our brains need to make sense of things, so we try to rationalize or justify something by searching for a reason or a lesson. Today, I do not believe that everything happens for reason. Sometimes things just happen.

There is no lesson to be learned from being beaten or abused. It does not happen for a reason – it is an evil thing that happens to people, and some are able to escape. There is no reason for being beaten as a child. Saying someone did not know any better is an excuse, not a reason.

Letting go of the idea that everything happens for a reason helped me learn how to forgive. I learned that there does not have to be a reason or a lesson for everything. Giving things purpose is a way that we make sense of the world, but we end up creating stories by giving purpose to things that do not need one.

My first journey with forgiveness was trying to understand that people do the best that they can at the time and that if I could learn to accept what had happened, I could move on. This was my original interpretation of forgiveness, but I did not learn the true power of forgiveness until I had my emotional healing breakthrough.

The first thing I learned was that what happened to me does not define me. I realized that what happened to me is not a reflection of who I am. Our actions and choices only define us if we continue to make them. They become part of us at the time, but people can change, and once we do those actions are no longer who we are.

As a society, we tend to judge other people based on the things they have done in the past. This does not define who that person is today. Judging someone like this indicates that you are not mentally well, and mental wellness is a big issue in the world today. I learned the power of forgiveness when I became mentally well.

The next thing I had to do was go through the steps to identify what was crippling me inside. As soon as I recognized what that was, I was able to start to forgive myself, and to this day I am able to experience true forgiveness naturally.

If you truly feel sorry about something you did, you will be able to forgive yourself. When someone else is not sorry about their actions and does not forgive themselves, you have the choice to decide what to do with it.

Betrayal is where I have found this the most. We often hear about broken marriages where one partner had an affair and left the marriage for another person, and they are not sorry about it. Saying, "I am sorry I hurt you" does not mean you are sorry. If someone is unfaithful and is sorry about it, they will go through the steps to address it and work through it instead of blaming their partner for driving them to an affair.

This brings up another point - Someone does not have to be sorry about what they did in order for you to forgive them. In fact, they never have to know that you have forgiven them. I have had very few conversations with people from my past where I told them I forgive them. No, forgiveness is something you do for yourself.

True healing and forgiveness need a witness and should be between you and someone that you trust. If you are a faith-based person, this could be between you and God. For others, it could mean talking to a professional who is trained to identify these thoughts and working through it with them.

I have used both the power of prayer and working through things with another human in my healing process. For years, I have prayed to God daily because I believe that God can do things for me no one else can. No matter what you call God, whether it is spirit or a mango tree, God can do for you what you cannot do for yourself. The power of prayer has been able to help me often with the ability to forgive.

Turning Your Fear Into Bravery

In previous chapters, I talked about fear and the ability fear has to paralyze us. Fear happens because our body is alerting us to danger and triggering our fight or flight response to help us survive.

However, fear can also cause us to become afraid of things that have nothing to do with our livelihoods. Self-doubt and negative self-talk can trap us, paralyzing us into settling for familiarity even when that familiarity is dangerous or uncomfortable.

We have these perceptions based on the stories we have heard or the experiences we have gone through since childhood. As children, we do not have a logical way to process the world around us, so we try to make some sense of the world in any way we can. If they are reinforced enough, the stories and narratives we are told as children can become our truth, whether they are real or rational or not.

This shifts away from the idea of perception and toward the notion of a learned experience that we tell ourselves is true.

For example, if you are used to being treated a certain way, whether it is negative or positive, it can cause fear when that individual stops treating you that way. You become used to the idea that if you do one thing, you will get a specific reaction from the other person. However, if that person is changing, that action will no longer trigger that same reaction, and even if you are happy a negative action is gone, it can cause fear because this is how you had become accustomed to getting that person's attention. You become afraid that the person is going to abandon you or reject you because they are no longer giving you the same attention.

Think of it in the way that people act out to get attention. Bad attention is better than no attention at all, so we continue to allow people to treat us terribly. As an adult, we allow ourselves to be treated the way we think we deserve to be treated. We have discussed this in previous chapters at length, but we teach others how to treat us through the way we act and react.

This is where we need to rely on our courage to turn into bravery. We need to become brave to be able to walk through our fears.

It takes courage to leave an abusive relationship, but sometimes courage alone is not enough. Sometimes we are afraid of losing everything. I work with abused women on a volunteer basis who tell me all the time that they are afraid to go to a shelter because they are afraid that they will lose their children or their house. If you end up dying from the abuse and the toll it takes, you will lose those things anyway, so you need to channel your fear into courage and bravery.

One thing I like to say is "Say what it is and add, 'So what.' If you cannot answer the "so what", then it is nothing." You can apply this to any challenge you are facing or decision you need to make to determine the magnitude. The answer will either bring you acceptance or a solution, but either way, you will be okay.

It may seem like a simple concept, but those two words can be life changing. The so what, and, or else – these are things you can say that are so simple but have a powerful effect. If I had learned this at 18, I would have lived a much different life.

To take your first step toward courage and bravery, you need to make one decision: you need to remove the "so what." When you do, it will come down to thoughts such as "I do not want to feel like this anymore," "I want to be loved," or "I want to be happy." If you feel like something if missing, you must make the decision to do something different. You must change whatever it is you are doing. If you are not happy, you need to evaluate your situation.

It all comes back to who are you inside? Who are you? Who is the real you? Who are you before society molded you to be whoever you think you are today? Are you chasing the right dreams? When you figure out who you really are inside, the rest falls into place. You will not accept anything that deviates from letting you be who you are, because that is the true joy. Be brave enough to discover who you really are and admit it.

True bravery is not letting fear stop you from acting. If you can overcome the fear, move into action through bravery. By getting brave, you will walk through fear gracefully.

To be brave is to be able to walk through fear with grace.

I hope that you find the power to be brave in your own life and take the next step towards truly healing and forgiving yourself. It took me a long time, but I have learned to forgive myself and let the rest of the pieces fall into place.

Chapter 10:

Boundaries

*"It is necessary, and even vital, to set standards for
your life and the people you allow in it."*
Mandy Hale

I never realized how healthy and peace-creating
boundaries could be until I started to place them in
my life. I thought I had to accept and allow people
to treat me badly, and that, somehow, I deserved whatever
I got.

I am glad that I finally learned my value and began the
process of developing and upholding healthy boundaries.
My life is so different now. Saying it is like night and day
does not begin to describe the difference. I can now
recognize bad and hurtful behavior and say, "No more!" I
get to decide where to draw the line. If everyone could set

healthy boundaries from the start, we would be able to save ourselves a lot of pain and agony.

When it comes to intimate and romantic relationships, and even friendships, to set healthy boundaries, you have to take time to get to know someone. So many people rush into relationships (especially romantic ones) and forget to take the time to learn where your boundaries are being challenged and even violated.

When you know how to set healthy boundaries, it becomes second nature, so when someone makes you uncomfortable, it becomes an internal red flag. You start to think, "Hmmm, I do not like how this person is talking to me. I think they are going to cause me some trouble later."

This applies to any type of relationship, whether it is a romantic relationship, co-worker relationship, or even a parent-child relationship. Every relationship needs healthy boundaries, but society often teaches us to violate those boundaries.

For example, one of the most common parent-child boundaries happens when children do not want to hug others, but parents force them to. They tell their kids to hug friends, relatives, or others goodbye, and if the child expresses, they are not comfortable doing so, the parent will tell them they have to. They will say, "Give your aunt a hug goodbye," even if the child does not want to.

If anyone does not feel comfortable hugging someone, no matter their age, this physical boundary should be respected. Children are being taught at a young age how to allow others to violate their boundaries.

Boundaries are tied to emotions. Sometimes, people with solid boundaries in place get mislabeled as aggressive or mean when they are being assertive and hold those boundaries in place. Stating what you want calmly and firmly does not mean you are mean, but some people might see it that way. They cannot roll over you because you stand up for yourself and that makes the other person uncomfortable.

For the longest time, I cared so much about what people thought that I would move my own boundaries for comfort and convenience. I thought if I adjusted my boundaries, people would love me.

Many people do this. You move your boundaries just to be accepted, included, or loved. It even happens as parents with their children and can be exemplified in divorced relationships.

That is why it takes time to set healthy boundaries. However, you must understand how to identify those boundaries before you can start to implement them.

How to Set Good Boundaries

I grew up in a family that had vibrant and loud conversations at the dinner table. No topics were off limits. One year, I met a friend at camp who lived further away, and I spent the weekend at her house. I learned that in her family, dinner time was silent. It was supposed to be her father's quiet time, so no one said a word during dinner. It made me uncomfortable, and I did not like it. When I told my mom about it, she told me if I did not like it then I did not have to go back. It was as simple as that – I set a boundary because something made me uncomfortable.

It comes down to your intuition. You need to be in touch with your mind, your gut, and your heart. If something does not feel right, you need to explore that. It is important to figure out why something is making you feel uncomfortable to set the right boundaries and remedy the situation.

Setting new boundaries is much harder than building on boundaries you have already established. Pre-existing boundaries give you a foundation to build on, while setting new ones requires more time and dedication.

Everyone is unique, but there are certain processes you can follow to set boundaries in different situations. No matter who you are, it is helpful to start with exploring the things that make you uncomfortable.

There are two basic types of boundaries: emotional and physical. Each one has an impact on your mental health and emotional well-being.

Physical Boundaries: The Barrier to Well-Being

Physical boundaries are a good starting place for boundary-setting because it is easier to identify physical things that make you uncomfortable. Whether that is an uncomfortable hug or an invasion of personal space, you can tell when you do not feel comfortable with someone's actions.

A common boundary is when someone gets too close to you when talking. For most people, the natural instinct is to take a step back when they get too far into your personal space. There are people who you are comfortable with when they get close to you and you do not feel your boundaries being pushed, while you may withdraw at other times. You communicate this through body language.

Violating physical boundaries can easily affect your well-being. Everyone has their own physical boundaries, and it is important to recognize your comfort zone. As a society, it is important to teach each other to respect our comfort zones and physical boundaries. Think about what makes you uncomfortable, whether it is at the grocery store, with friends or family, or in a social group, and ask yourself, "What boundaries do I need?"

Physical boundaries tend to be easier to enforce than emotional boundaries. If someone gets too close to you and makes you uncomfortable, you can simply back away or avoid them entirely.

The healthiest thing to do is to hold that boundary with someone who is making you uncomfortable and communicate with them. It is okay to tell someone, "I do not like doing this" or "I like this, but…" You do not have to protect their feelings because you are taking care of yourself. Say it in a respectful way; if that person has a problem with it, it is their problem, not yours.

When you have a healthy boundary system, it does not matter how well you know someone. You can still back away to protect your boundaries and use strong communication skills to get the point across.

Emotional Boundaries: Letting Go of Your Shame and Guilt

Emotional boundaries are more difficult to implement and identify because they do not always directly correlate with one specific action, or you may not realize they are impacting your life. They are also more difficult to hold.

Emotional and intellectual boundaries have a direct impact on your self-esteem. When those boundaries are not well protected, they can damage your mental health. This becomes evident when you start to feel like you are not enough or not good enough.

Those feelings can be repaired when you put up strong emotional boundaries. They are how you create and identify yourself so that other people can behave how you need them to. This way, you can decide what types of communication and behaviors are acceptable.

It is easier to maintain and put up boundaries with people who are emotionally healthy. However, most people have weak or poor boundaries and have trouble separating their feelings from others, which is where poor self-esteem comes in.

With weak emotional boundaries, you become raw and expose yourself to being vulnerable to other people's words and actions. This is how you get hurt or feel

151

wounded. Anything can have a deep effect, from someone's actions or choices to their beliefs or behaviors.

Happiness and sadness are also affected by personal boundaries. If you are with someone who is sad, you may pick up on their level of emotion. You may even be tempted to sacrifice your plans or goals to please others because you do not have boundaries in place.

Blaming others for your problems is a big factor. If you keep blaming others for your problems, you will not be able to take action and fix them.

This question comes up often in my work: We do not want our boundaries violated, and it does not feel good when that happens, so why do so many of us ignore what we need by not upholding them or not setting them in the first place?

In my experience, most of the time it is out of fear of abandonment or rejection. There is also a fear of confrontation. You might be afraid to tell someone they are violating your boundaries because you are afraid that they will become angry and retaliate.

That feeling is guilt. Sometimes you do not honor or maintain your boundaries properly because of guilt. Too often, you are afraid to tell people how you feel because you are afraid of offending or upsetting them, and you were not taught how to properly set and hold boundaries in your life.

The Power of Boundaries

You might panic when setting strong boundaries because you experience a conflict when someone violates those boundaries. If you try to create boundaries without help, it can become overwhelming and you might end up turning everything into a boundary. This works both ways, like a swinging pendulum: you can go from setting little or no boundaries and then set too many, and sometimes inappropriate boundaries in one sweeping motion.

When you start to put new boundaries into place, some people will feel you are changing the rules and will not like it. They may work hard to drag you back into your old way of behaving. That is okay; maintain your guidelines for self-respect and self-love. Not everyone will like what you do nor the boundaries you set, but boundaries are a part of your identity. They shape who you are.

As I mentioned, setting boundaries with someone is the way to build mutual trust. I used to rush into relationships thinking I needed to immediately share intimate stories and past incidents. Being vulnerable to a fault was my modus operando, moving from one intimate relationship to another. I have since learned that was a sign, a big red flag, that I lacked healthy boundary setting. You should share personal information with others gradually, over time, to develop real sharing and trusting relationships.

Unhealthy boundaries come from sharing too much information too soon. Closing yourself off and not expressing your needs and wants is also a boundary violation. If you are afraid to say no because you are afraid of rejection or abandonment, even though that is what you mean, you are going to experience impostor syndrome. Before you notice it, you will start to feel like you are not good enough because people are rejecting your difference of opinion.

In a true and equal partnership, both partners share power and responsibility. That means setting great boundaries between you. You both need to be able to say "Yes" or "No" with confidence and know it will be okay. You also need to be able to separate your needs and desires from one another.

Everyone's boundaries are different, and that does not mean that one person is better than the other. You might carry so much shame that this concept can be difficult to understand and challenging to implement.

Healthy boundaries empower you to make healthy choices and take responsibility for yourself. You are not responsible for someone else's happiness. You decide your own self-worth based on how you let others treat you. When you stop letting other people make decisions for you and have boundaries in place, you begin to feel responsible and develop a sense of control over your life.

Create Your Action Plan and Learn to Say No

Do you know that "No" is a complete sentence? I cannot tell you how many years I thought using the word "No" needed an explanation or excuse. If you are curious about how to put better boundaries in your life, I will share my high-level rules for doing so.

First, you must do it clearly, calmly, and respectfully. It should also be short. Avoid justifying your boundary or building a story around it. When you are ready to communicate your boundaries, do not apologize for your boundary setting. For example, do not say, "I am sorry. I know this is going to upset you, but I cannot…" This is not a boundary.

Learning to say "No" is the most important boundary to start with. When you do not say "No," you end up with complications down the road.

This was my problem: I used to say "Yes" to everything. I had young children, and I knew I could get jobs and tasks done better than anyone else without complaint. Anytime someone would ask for a volunteer for something, my hand was always the first to go up. Before I knew it, I would have a full plate. I would always get the tasks done, but I never gave myself time to enjoy things I wanted to do. For that reason, I never got the chance to figure out what I enjoyed doing because I was always doing things for others.

When you are learning how to say "No," you can start by buying time. If someone asks you to do something or requests something from you, say, "Let me think about it." You do not have to give an immediate answer, and you do not owe anyone an explanation. You are not responsible for how the other person reacts. You are only responsible for communicating what you need.

If you do upset someone, understand that it is their problem, especially if that person is manipulating or controlling you. They are going to test you, and you will need to be prepared.

When setting boundaries with someone who is manipulating or controlling you, start slowly, and do not rush into it. If you try to rush it, you could end up putting yourself in a dangerous situation.

This will not be easy in abusive situations, but you can do it. Expect backlash and be prepared to remain firm regardless of how they react. If your behavior does not match the boundary you are setting, you cannot establish a clear boundary. This sends mixed messages, and anyone you attempt to set the boundary with will try to push it and test it because it is uncomfortable for them.

When setting boundaries in an abusive situation where they might threaten your physical safety, it is best to do this with the assistance of a professional. You need to create a safety plan or an escape plan, and if you do not work with a coach, therapist, counsellor, or advocate, the outcome could be deadly. Your boundaries are there to protect you. They should be a part of your safety plan.

As I said, setting boundaries will not be easy, but I want you to know it is completely natural to feel selfish, guilty, or embarrassed when you are setting a new boundary for the first time. It will be uncomfortable, but you need to do it anyway.

I consider myself to be good at setting boundaries now. I can recognize when I need to set a boundary or when a boundary is being violated. However, it took me a long time to get there.

You have the right to self-care, and setting boundaries requires practice and determination. It is important to learn not to let anxiety, fear, and guilt prevent you from taking care of yourself. For women, this can be increasingly difficult because we are so used to taking care of everyone else that we often forget to take care of ourselves. However, taking care of yourself means setting clear, healthy boundaries.

Another important part of setting boundaries is understanding how you feel. If you feel angry or resentful toward someone or something, or if you find yourself complaining or whining about something, it is a good sign you need a boundary.

Everything you do on your journey toward healing and recovery will lead you to setting healthy boundaries. It is a process that takes time. You need to complete the process on your own time, not when someone else tells you to.

Another good rule of thumb is to eliminate toxic people from your life. Get rid of anyone in your life who wants to manipulate, control, or use you. No matter who it is, whether it is a co-worker, a partner, or a friend, they are only going to continue reducing your self-worth. If you do not cut them out of your life, you will not be able to keep enough boundaries.

It is a privilege for other people to be in your life. Emotions can overwhelm you and if you do not have healthy boundaries in place, they can become difficult to sort out or navigate. That is when life can start to feel like chaos.

The idea of outgrowing relationships, no matter what kind, is also scary. Remember that it is okay to feel like this, but the only way to create a joyful and fulfilling life is to decide what and who you allow into it.

If setting boundaries is challenging for you like it is for many people, there is help. Inside my private and free Facebook group – Bridges2Bravery – you can download free workbooks and get other free tools to help you.

Shari Lueck

Chapter 11:

The Skeletons Have Changed

"Find ecstasy in life: the mere sense of living is joy enough."

Emily Dickinson

What a journey this has been. Writing this book has been one of revelation, joy, overwhelm, grief, and occasionally sadness. Going back and revisiting the good, bad, and ugly in my life stirred up a lot of emotions and led me to visit old ways of thinking I no longer need. It was not always easy, but it was worth it.

The life I now live is incredible and, as my husband says when someone asks him how he is, "almost perfect." Like everyone reading this, there are still days I struggle and days my emotions are out of whack. But now those struggles do not take me out or drag me down a rabbit hole. Instead, they provide opportunities for growth and acceptance. I have learned to recognize when my old way of thinking and the things from my past try to creep back in to hurt me, and now I stop, practice the pause, and deal with them.

In this last chapter I want to share my methodology for healing the past and creating a life that you not only desire but deserve. First, I want to make it clear I am not a licensed medical professional. I am a Certified Life Coach and NLP practitioner who is sharing what has worked in my life and for hundreds of clients.

You may have things in your life right now that require the help of a licensed medical professional. If you do, there is no shame in that. Please get the help you need and start the process of being set free. Most of these ideas I am going to share with you should also help.

The ARC Methodology: Three Simple Steps

By now, you know I spent years searching for healing and relief. I tried doctors, therapy, and recovery groups. My breakthrough (and ultimate transformation) was so incredible that I committed to helping others.

After years of participating in and studying the different modalities and variety of coaching methods and techniques available, I designed the ARC methodology. This unique and simple three-step program is designed from the studies, certifications, NLP training, and science that led me to love my life and become the person I am today.

The ARC methodology can be defined in three words: "A" stands for Admit (identify), "R" stands for Review, and "C" stands for Choose/Create, which ultimately means healing. Each step has sub-steps, but these three steps are the core components.

You do not have to drudge through the past, but you do need to identify what is holding you back. Once you identify what is in your way and creating limiting beliefs in your life, you can admit how they serve you and how they hurt you. Then you can review the stories you tell yourself and the coping mechanisms you have adopted. You can rewrite your story and choose what you want and change who you are so you can finally heal.

My method works quickly. People are often amazed that, in less than 60 minutes, my clients say they feel hopeful, relieved, peaceful, and educated on what they need to do next. Anyone who takes one of my classes comes out a different person.

This is how I came up with the business name for my integrative, breakthrough coaching business – Bridges2Bravery.

If you are ready to cross that bridge and want to transform your life, you will not regret it. You are never too old, too young, or too late to start. To learn more about me and how I can help you cross that bridge, please visit www.sharilueck.com

Conclusion

Everything does not happen for a reason, but your past hardships are the barriers to uncovering who you are.

I still have nightmares. They are not the same as the ones I had as a child, but at 55, I can still wake up from screaming in terror in my sleep.

At times, I have flashbacks that transport me to different spots in hell that I have walked through over the course of my lifetime. Grounded in the reality of what my life is today does not minimize my experiences nor does it justify the horror of my past. But not everything happens for a reason, nor is there a lesson in the trauma. However, I can choose how I react and remember.

Acts of hate and division still trigger me. The senseless violence erupting across the nation and news of senseless murder victims killed for their beliefs or color of their skin can stop me in my tracks. I can still feel the icy horror and sheer terror in the exact moment I arrived on scene following the news that my children's school had been the scene of a mass shooting. I can remember the fear I had when I was told my son was transported to Children's Hospital by helicopter and the absence of relief when I learned it was a different boy. I can still see the evil man, Buford Furrow, after his arrest proclaiming that he was there "to kill the next generation of Jews."

When I learn of abuse of others, either physical or emotional, I feel the fear and discomfort that lingered for so long inside me. To this day, I do not like elevated voices or yelling but anger no longer frightens me. I choose to feed the love and hope inside me that led me here and will always lead me forward.

Looking back and remembering the times I was shackled to the fear, shame, guilt, anger, and resentment of my past no longer paralyzes me. I am equipped to face the reality of the here and now and remember that none of that defines me. The fact that I have always had the ability to choose hope and love regardless of the horror is a gift I have always been blessed with.

Some call it resilience, and the evolution of grit, but for me it is my gift. There are some things that happen in life that we are powerless over. The fear I carried following the hate crime in 1999 that my children would not survive. The terror watching the towers fall on 9/11. The coronavirus attacking the immunocompromised and fearing my son with MS would not see his 23rd birthday. Reading about or hearing leaders of our great country divide and spew hate. There can be pervasive fear for those who have survived trauma and have been scarred with PTSD.

Today I am empowered by my mind's ability to choose. I can reflect on my time in hell and clearly see the inner strength I had to push forward and keep on going. I discovered parts of me I would have never known existed had I not had the experiences that shaped me.

You have this ability and the capacity to choose. When it seems like nothing helpful or beneficial is available on the outside, that is the time to turn inward and discover who you are. It is not what happens to you that defines you nor matters most; it is what you do with those experiences that matters.

When you escape the prison in your mind, you become free from the things that hold you back and learn to trust yourself. No matter how great your suffering is or how strong the prison bars of your mind, it is possible to break free from whatever is holding you back.

It is not always easy, but it is always worth it!

I do not want people to read my story and think, "There is no way my suffering compares to hers." Instead, I want people to read my story and think, "If she can do it, so can I."

You do not change until you are ready. Sometimes, readiness comes from a difficult situation or tough circumstances, like divorce, death, illness, or an accident. There is a pull forcing you to face up to what is not working and try something else. Other times, it is your inner pain and lack of fulfillment that becomes so persistent and loud you cannot ignore it any longer.

Just because something is bad does not mean you are ready. I get asked all the time, "Why did you stay in an abusive marriage? Why did you keep going back?" Readiness to change does not come from the outside. It cannot be rushed or forced. Readiness comes from within. You are ready when something shifts on the inside and you decide.

Change is about interrupting the habits, patterns, and thinking that no longer serve you. If you want to meaningfully alter your life, you do not simply abandon a dysfunctional belief or habit. Instead, you choose what you are moving toward.

As you begin your journey to freedom, it is important to reflect not only on what you want to be free from, but on what you want to be free to do. The purpose of changing your life is not to become a new you; it is to become the real you – the *you* that God created you to be.

Everything that has happened to you, the choices you have made, and all the ways you tried to cope and survive are all useful. Forgiveness and change do not mean you have to throw away everything up until this point and start from scratch. Whatever you have done, whether by choice or by chance, brought you this far. You are exactly where you are supposed to be and you deserve to be happy, joyous, and free.

If this book has helped you in any way, then I have accomplished my goal. My dream has always been and still is to help people live better lives. Go to www.sharilueck.com and check out my free resources. They are designed to help you start your journey today.

Now is YOUR time. Do not be afraid to take that first step and walk on to your Bridge2Bravery. It may feel hard and a bit scary at first, but later when you look back, you will be thankful that you named your skeletons and they no longer scare you nor have power over you.

Shari Lueck

Works Cited

A.A. World Services Inc. *Alcoholics Anonymous, 4th Edition*. A.A. World Services Inc., 1939. Hardcover.

Engel, Beverly L.M.F.T. *Healing Your Shame and Guilt Through Self-Forgiveness*. 1 June 2017. article. 16 10 2020.

Greater Good Magazine. *https://greatergood.berkeley.edu/topic/forgiveness/definition*. n.d. 14 October 2020.

Kallal, Leanne. *https://tinybuddha.com/blog/a-simple-process-to-turn-fear-into-power/*. n.d. webpage. 16 10 2020.

Lawrence Robinson and Melinda Smith, M.A. *https://www.helpguide.org/articles/anxiety/dealing-with-uncertainty.htm*. April 2020. webpage. 16 October 2020.

Lawrence Robinson, Melinda Smith, M.A., and Jeanne Segal, Ph.D. *https://www.helpguide.org/articles/anxiety/how-to-stop-worrying.htm*. September 2020. webpage. 16 10 2020.

Made in the USA
Monee, IL
12 November 2020